D1254258

SPORTS STARS WITH HEART
Steve Nash
LEADER ON AND OFF THE COURT

by Ryan Basen

Enslow Publishers, Inc.
40 Industrial Road
Box 398
Berkeley Heights, NJ 07922
USA
http://www.enslow.com

Library of Congress Cataloging-in-Publication Data
Basen, Ryan.
  Steve Nash : leader on and off the court / by Ryan Basen.
     p. cm.—(Sports stars with heart)
  Includes bibliographical references and index.
  ISBN-13: 978-0-7660-2868-5
  ISBN-10: 0-7660-2868-2
  1. Nash, Steve, 1974—Juvenile literature. 2. Basketball players—
Canada—Biography—Juvenile literature. I. Title.
  GV884.N36B37 2007
  796.357092—dc22
     [B]   2006031844

Credits

Editorial Direction: Red Line Editorial, Inc. (Bob Temple)
Editor: Sue Green
Design and Page Production: The Design Lab

Printed in the United States of America

10 9 8 7 6 5 4 3 2 1

To Our Readers: We have done our best to make sure all Internet addresses in this book were active and appropriate when we went to press. However, the author and the publisher have no control over and assume no liability for the material available on those Internet sites or on other Web sites they may link to. Any comments or suggestions can be sent by e-mail to comments@enslow.com or to the address on the back cover.

Photographs © 2007: AP Photo/Roberto Borea: 23; AP Photo/Paul Connors: 4, 12, 109; AP Photo/Kevork Djansezian: 40; AP Photo/Gloria Ferniz: 73; AP Photo/Kevin Frayer: 3, 51; AP Photo/Eric Gay: 1; AP Photo/Jeff T. Green: 18; AP Photo/Tony Gutierrez: 91; AP Photo/Aaron Harris: 47; AP Photo/Tom Hood: 81; AP Photo/Kent Horner: 57; AP Photo/Bill Janscha: 68; AP Photo/Erik S. Lesser: 3; AP PHOTO/CP, Vancouver Sun-Ian Lindsay: 79; AP Photo/Donna McWilliam: 3, 45, 89, 99; AP Photo/Rich Pedroncelli: 71; AP Photo/Elaine Thompson: 102; AP Photo/Kathy Willens: 32; AP Photo/Adrian Wyld: 77; AP Photo/Steve Yeater: 65; AP Photo/Matt York: 7, 97

Cover Photo: Steve Nash goes to the basket in Game 5 of the NBA Western Conference Finals June 1, 2006, in Dallas, Texas.

CONTENTS

Steve Nash clutches the 2006 NBA MVP trophy.

CHAPTER ONE

Keeping His Cool

Early on the evening of May 8, 2006, Steve Nash stood near half court inside Phoenix's US Airways Center and looked at David Stern, the commissioner of the National Basketball Association (NBA). Stern then handed Nash the NBA's Most Valuable Player (MVP) trophy for the second straight season.

As the Phoenix Suns point guard hoisted the trophy, the crowd of about 18,000 stood and cheered. Nash celebrated the honor by scoring 31 points and earning 12 assists as the Suns beat the Los Angeles Clippers 130–123 in Game 1 of an NBA Western Conference semifinal.

A WILD RIDE

The events of May 8 were just part of a wild spring for Nash, one of the NBA's most unlikely superstars.

In a span of just over two weeks, Nash led the Suns back from a three-games-to-one deficit in the first round of the playoffs to beat the Los Angeles Lakers, became only the ninth player in NBA history to win consecutive MVP awards, and directed the Suns to another seven-game series victory, this time against the Clippers. Nash was also named one of *Time Magazine*'s 100 People Who Shape Our World.

"I have to pinch myself," he said about winning the 2005–06 NBA MVP award. "I couldn't believe it last year, and to do it again is even more difficult to understand."[1]

DID YOU KNOW?

Nash is one of only nine players in NBA history to win back-to-back NBA regular season MVP awards.

The others were: Tim Duncan (2001–02 and 2002–03), Michael Jordan (1990–91 and 1991–92), Magic Johnson (1988–89 and 1989–90), Larry Bird (1983–84, 1984–85, and 1985–86), Moses Malone (1981–82 and 1982–83), Kareem Abdul-Jabbar (1970–71 and 1971–72; and 1975–76 and 1976–77), Wilt Chamberlain (1965–66, 1966–67, and 1967–68), and Bill Russell (1960–61, 1961–62, and 1962–63).

Throughout all of that drama, Nash remained calm as usual. The six-foot three-inch, 195-pound Canadian native continued to control games usually ruled by much bigger men. He led one of the NBA's best teams. During the first two rounds of the 2006

NBA Playoffs, Nash averaged 20.2 points and a team-high 10.2 assists per game.

That followed a regular season during which Nash set career highs by averaging 18.8 points and 4.2 rebounds per game. He led the league in free-throw shooting with an average of 92.1 percent. Nash also led the NBA with 10.5 assists per game, helping the Suns win a second straight Pacific Division title with a 54–28 record. Five other Suns set career highs in points per game during the season, an incredible statistic that many experts attributed to Nash's brilliance.

Nash reacts to his team's efforts in the conference finals.

"Steve is not just a great player," said Suns chairman Jerry Colangelo. "He's one of the few players who I believe have ever played who makes everyone better around him."[2]

Nash especially asserted his control during must-win games that the Suns played early in the 2006

NBA Playoffs. In the first-round series against the Lakers, the Suns trailed 3–2. In Game 6, Nash scored 32 points and tallied 13 assists as the Suns won 126–118 in overtime. In the second round against the Clippers, the series was tied 3–3. In Game 7, Nash made 11 of 16 shots on his way to scoring 29 points. He added 11 assists as the Suns won 127–107.

Nash played well despite battling several minor injuries. As the Suns prepared to face the Dallas Mavericks in the Western Conference Finals, sportswriters and other experts had even begun to talk about the thirty-two-year-old as a candidate for the Basketball Hall of Fame—once he retires, of course. But to somebody who loves basketball as much as Nash, retirement will not come soon.

STEVE NASH'S BIO

Born: Johannesburg, South Africa, February 7, 1974, grew up in Victoria, British Columbia (Canada)

Height: 6' 3"

Weight: 195 pounds

Team: Phoenix Suns

Previous Teams: Dallas Mavericks, Phoenix Suns

Position: Guard

Off the court: Nash runs a foundation for underserved kids and funds a youth basketball league in Vancouver, B.C.

NOT A TYPICAL NBA STAR

Nash has been called the unlikeliest of NBA superstars because of the many obstacles he has had to overcome to reach such an elite level. He is not very big for an NBA player. He played

NASH'S BASKETBALL TIMELINE

1980s: Played basketball growing up in Victoria. Joined first organized basketball league in eighth grade.

1988–92: St. Michael's University School, Victoria

1992–96: Santa Clara University in California

1996–98: Phoenix Suns

1998–2004: Dallas Mavericks

2004–present: Phoenix Suns

at Santa Clara, a small college in California, against mediocre competition. He grew up in Canada, a country that has produced few other NBA players. In fact, Nash never even played organized basketball until the eighth grade.

"People have always told me that I'd fall on my face, that I wouldn't make it this far," Nash said. "But here I am."[3]

Despite all of those barriers, Nash has become one of the NBA's best players. He sets an example for younger players with his work ethic. He drives by much bigger, quicker players, keeping his dribble for what seems like hours. He hits tough floaters over big men in the lane and regularly nails outside jump shots over taller guards.

NASH'S NBA TRANSACTIONS
- **June 26, 1996: Picked in first round of the NBA Draft by the Phoenix Suns (No. 15 overall)**
- **June 24, 1998: Traded to Dallas Mavericks for Pat Garrity, Bubba Wells, Martin Muursepp, and a 1999 first-round pick (Shawn Marion)**
- **July 14, 2004: Signed as free agent with the Suns**

"He can shoot it from anywhere," said Steve Francis, the New York Knicks guard, "and he never picks up his dribble."[4]

"Going 100 miles per hour all the time—that's his game," said Dirk Nowitzki, one of Nash's best friends and a former Mavericks teammate.[5]

"When you have a point guard who can pass as well as he can, it makes the game a lot easier," said Amare Stoudemire, a Suns forward.[6]

Nash became a dominant player through determination, hard work, consistency, and a calm, cool personality. "You just can't startle him," said Loy Vaught, who played with Nash on the Mavericks during the 2000–01 season. "When you see Steve Nash, the first thing that pops into your head is, 'cool.'"[7]

Playing with a leader that cool gave the Suns plenty of confidence as they prepared for the Western Conference Finals. They were just two series victories from doing the one big thing Nash has never done in his ten-year NBA career: win an NBA championship.

To anybody who knew Steve Nash when he was growing up as a skinny kid in western Canada, leading a team to an NBA title would be an unbelievable accomplishment.

CHAPTER TWO

A Gifted Athlete

Steve Nash has made his mark as an NBA player in Phoenix and Dallas, two thriving Sunbelt cities. No matter how much time he spends in the United States, though, Nash still relates more to another country: Canada.

Stephen John Nash, the oldest child of John and Jean Nash, was born on February 7, 1974, in Johannesburg, the largest city in South Africa. He did not live there for very long.

Before Steve turned two years old, the Nashes moved across the Atlantic Ocean. They first settled in Regina, the capital of the Canadian province of Saskatchewan. Then they moved to Vancouver, the largest city in the Canadian province of British Columbia. The Nashes finally settled for good in Victoria, a scenic city located just south of Vancouver.

John Nash at his son Steve's game

A SPORTS-LOVING FAMILY

John Nash worked in Victoria as a marketing manager. Jean Nash became a special-needs assistant at a local elementary school. They had two more children after Steve: Martin and Joann.

The three Nash children grew up loving sports. Steve played organized soccer, hockey, lacrosse, rugby, baseball, and other sports. His best sport growing up may have been soccer, continuing the family tradition. His father was once a semipro soccer player. The Nash family's favorite sports team for years has been the Tottenham Hotspur, a Premier League soccer team in London, England. John Nash is originally from England.

"My dad, my grandfather, and my uncle grew up watching them," Steve said. "That's tradition. They tell me I play net ball. They say it's (basketball), a girls' game."[1]

Steve excelled in many other sports as a kid. He was the starting fullback, for example, on a high school rugby team that won a British Columbia provincial championship. That is similar to a state championship in U.S. high school sports.

GETTING SERIOUS ABOUT BASKETBALL

Steve only dabbled in basketball for much of his childhood. When some of his friends started playing basketball competitively, though, he joined them. He played in an organized league for the first time in the eighth grade.

He immediately fell in love with the sport and caught on to it quickly. Like soccer, it involved a

VICTORIA

Capital of British Columbia, a province in Canada

Population: 325,000

Location: twenty miles north of the border between Canada and the United States, on the southern tip of Vancouver Island. Victoria is a short ferry ride from Seattle, Washington, and Vancouver, British Columbia.

Nickname: Garden City

Other famous natives: singer Nelly Furtado, former NHL players Russ and Geoff Courtnall

TOTTENHAM HOTSPUR FACTS

- The Hotspur is the favorite soccer team of the Nash family, including Steve.
- Tottenham is a borough of London, England's capital city, and is the hometown of John Nash, Steve's father.
- Tottenham plays in England's Premier League, one of the top soccer leagues in the world. It is one of seven Premiership teams playing in greater London. Chelsea, Arsenal, Charlton Athletic, Fulham, West Ham United, and Watford are the others.

ST. MICHAEL'S UNIVERSITY SCHOOL FACTS

Private school, K-12

Location: Victoria

Enrollment: 890

15 varsity sports, including boys' basketball

Athletics Director: Ian Hyde-Lay (Steve Nash's high school basketball coach)

lot of positioning and dribbling. He began to master the latter skill. Steve enrolled as a high school student at St. Michael's University School, a small private school in Victoria. He became the school team's starting point guard and its top player.

By grade twelve, Steve was a star. He averaged more than 21 points, 9 rebounds, and 11 assists per game and led St. Michael's to the provincial championship.

Steve realized how talented he was and how much he loved basketball. He set a personal goal. One day he would play in the NBA. Such a goal was almost unheard of in Canada. Dozens of professional hockey players grow up in the country, but only a few players in the history of the NBA have been Canadian natives.

That was in part because Canada did not have a college basketball system as competitive as that in the United States.

"After high school, Canada doesn't really have a next level," Steve said. "Not enough kids, not enough tradition."[2]

Steve knew that in order to make it to the NBA his best option would be to move to the United States and play college basketball.

TESTING HIS TALENT

Steve warmed up for that move as a high school student by playing against top American high school players in summer tournaments in Long Beach, California, and Las Vegas, Nevada. He also met with Tim Hardaway, then an All-Star guard with the NBA's Golden State Warriors, to learn about weight lifting. In addition, Steve spent one summer in Seattle, Washington, playing competitive basketball while living with a friend's family.

That summer he would dribble a basketball wherever he went, prompting his friend's grandmother to call the ball "Steve's girlfriend."[3] Steve's goal was to improve his left-handed dribbling skills. Earlier, a coach at a basketball camp criticized him for not being better at that skill.

"That was the last time I was going to hear that," Steve said.[4]

TRYING TO ATTRACT ATTENTION

Steve continued to excel as he gained experience, proving to himself that he was good enough to play with a top American college basketball program. He set his sights on Syracuse and Washington. He mailed out

> ## "No one could keep up with him. Guys were falling all over the place."
>
> ### —Scott Gradin

tapes and letters to other American schools as well.

None of them wanted him. Why not? Perhaps they could not believe their own eyes. If the college coaches even bothered to watch the tapes, they saw highlights of Steve embarrassing defenders. He would dominate games and "break their ankles," making cross-over dribbles that caused opponents to stumble and sometimes even fall down.

"It made me laugh out loud," said Scott Gradin, an assistant who watched Steve's tapes. "No one could keep up with him. Guys were falling all over the place."[5]

Gradin was then a part-time assistant at Santa Clara, a small university near San Jose, California. Once he saw Steve's tape, he showed it to Dick Davey, another Santa Clara assistant.

Davey had to see Steve in person to believe what he saw on the tape. Davey went to Vancouver to watch Steve play in the British Columbia senior boys' AAA championships in the winter of 1992. Steve was terrific. He led St. Michael's to the title and was named tournament MVP. Davey knew then that Steve was good enough to play at Santa Clara—or at any American school.

"I'm hoping—praying—there are no big boys [big-time college coaches] there," Davey recalled of scouting Steve at that tournament. "Because if there are, they're going to have some interest in the guy and I'm going to be out of luck. We were the only ones there."[6]

Almost immediately, the Broncos offered Steve a scholarship. Steve had never even heard of Santa Clara. But with no other options to play at American schools, Steve signed a letter of intent to play for the Broncos.

The Broncos played in the West Coast Conference (WCC), a relatively unknown league with teams such as Gonzaga and Loyola Marymount. WCC games were rarely aired on television. WCC teams played in old gyms, often in front of small crowds. The competition in the conference was regarded as weaker than the power conferences such as the Big East.

Steve wanted to test himself against the competition in the stronger conferences, but he settled for playing in the WCC. Playing at Santa Clara

WEST COAST CONFERENCE FACTS

Abbreviation: WCC

Headquarters: San Bruno, California

Teams: Gonzaga, Santa Clara, Loyola Marymount, San Francisco, San Diego, Pepperdine, Portland, St. Mary's

Notable men's basketball alumni: Steve Nash (Santa Clara), Bo Kimble (Loyola Marymount), John Stockton (Gonzaga), Adam Morrison (Gonzaga), Doug Christie (Pepperdine)

The Utah Jazz's John Stockton holds a replica of his number 12 Gonzaga jersey during a ceremony retiring his number on February 18, 2004.

would hurt his chances of reaching his ultimate goal of playing in the NBA, but it would not crush them. It was not unheard of for a WCC player to make it, and even excel, in the NBA.

John Stockton, a small Gonzaga point guard similar in size and skills to Steve, was drafted into the NBA by the Utah Jazz. By 1992, Stockton was an All-Star, teaming with Jazz forward Karl Malone to make Utah a consistent NBA powerhouse.

Other WCC players who had made it to the NBA included Bo Kimble, a Loyola Marymount guard who was chosen eighth overall in the 1990 NBA Draft. Hank Gathers, Kimble's teammate at Loyola Marymount, would likely have been drafted by an NBA team that year, too, but he died tragically during a college game.

So, in the fall of 1992, Steve enrolled at Santa Clara, leaving Canada behind for a new life in the United States. Although he was a bit disappointed, he kept focused on chasing his dream of playing in the NBA.

"Honestly, I wish it would have been Syracuse or Washington," Nash said of his choice for playing college basketball.[7]

"The lack of response [from American colleges] hurt me, because I thought I was good enough that people would come knocking on my door. . . . It was like I was trapped in an elevator and I'm screaming, but nobody could hear me."[8]

It would not be the last time the so-called basketball experts would ignore or doubt Steve Nash. Yet time and time again, he would prove anyone who doubted his abilities was making a big mistake.

DID YOU KNOW?
Singer Nelly Furtado, who also grew up in Victoria, recently wrote a song that references Steve Nash. In one verse of her song "Promiscuous," Furtado wonders aloud: "Is your game MVP like Steve Nash?"

CHAPTER THREE

Becoming a Leader

Late in the summer of 1992, Steve Nash arrived on the campus of Santa Clara University as a confident, baby-faced eighteen-year-old freshman point guard. Nash thought he was good enough to play basketball at a more renowned school, so he figured it was just a matter of time before he would be the Broncos' starting point guard.

He quickly learned that nothing was assured in big-time basketball. Just as he had worked hard to become a top Canadian high school player, Nash would have to work to thrive on the American collegiate level.

PLAYING AT A HIGHER LEVEL

During Broncos' practices early in the season, Nash was often embarrassed by veterans, including the team's starting point guard. Nash wondered to himself if he was good enough to contribute to the team. When the season started in November, he was not in the Broncos' starting lineup.

Yet Nash continued to develop his game, becoming one of the hardest workers on the team. That paid off toward the end of the year. He became a starter and a key player for the Broncos.

Nash caught fire in the WCC Tournament. In the final against Pepperdine, he made 7 of 9 three-point attempts to score 23 points. He was named the tournament's MVP, and the Broncos won the title. That win secured a berth for Santa Clara in the NCAA Tournament.

PLAYING THE ROLE OF UNDERDOG

Only one team in each conference is guaranteed a spot in the NCAA Tournament. The so-called "power conferences," such as the ACC and Pac-10, usually earn several at-large NCAA Tournament bids. But small conferences such as the WCC rarely get any, so winning the conference

"Steve is really deranged."

–Dick Davey

tournament is often the only way a WCC team can make it into the NCAA Tournament.

That was the case in 1993. The Broncos were seeded No. 15 in the NCAA Tournament's West region. That meant they would have to play No. 2 seed Arizona in the first round.

The Wildcats had won the Pac-10 Conference in the regular season, going 17–1 against powerhouses such as UCLA and Cal. They were loaded with future NBA players, including guards Khalid Reeves and Damon Stoudamire and All-American forward Chris Mills.

Arizona's talent and depth, plus the fact that only one No. 15 seed had ever won an NCAA Tournament game, made Santa Clara a big underdog. That did not matter to the Broncos as they prepared for the game, held in Salt Lake City, Utah, on March 18.

Santa Clara built an early lead, but Arizona went on a 25–0 run and led by thirteen points early in the second half. Although they struggled shooting the ball, the Broncos managed to stay in the game. Mills sat out most of the second half with foul trouble. Suddenly Arizona went cold shooting the ball, and the Broncos seized the lead again.

In the final minute, the Wildcats had to foul the Broncos often to stop the clock as they tried to mount a comeback. They fouled Nash a few times. The freshman was so excited that each time he was

Mark Schmitz (20) and Steve Nash celebrate their team's win against Arizona during the NCAA basketball tournament.

fouled he ran to the free-throw line. He then composed himself and nailed the free throws.

In that final minute, Nash made six straight from the line. Although he missed a pair in the final seconds, the Broncos held off the Wildcats 64–61 when Stoudamire missed a long three-point attempt at the buzzer.

Nash was praised by the media and basketball experts after the game, which was called one of the biggest upsets in college basketball history. Tiny Santa

NO. 15 SEEDS TO WIN MEN'S BASKETBALL NCAA TOURNAMENT GAMES (ALL AGAINST NO. 2 SEEDS):

Richmond over Syracuse (1991)

Santa Clara over Arizona (1993)

Coppin State over South Carolina (1997)

Hampton over Iowa State (2001)

Clara had beaten Arizona. Nash's team became just the second No. 15 seed to win an NCAA Tournament game since the field expanded to 64 teams in 1985.

"We knew it was a possibility," Nash said. "But I don't think we realized it was going to happen until Damon Stoudamire's shot bounced off the rim."[1]

The Broncos lost their next game, falling 68–57 in the second round to Temple to end their season. But the win against Arizona set the foundation for an excellent four years for Nash at Santa Clara.

HIGH HOPES

After 1993, the Broncos had new expectations. Their goals now were to win the WCC and compete in the NCAA Tournament.

Nash's sophomore year was a transition season. The Broncos lost several players from their 1992–93 squad to graduation. They needed the young Nash to be a team leader. He was up for the challenge.

Nash led the Broncos in scoring, averaging 14.6 points per game, and set a school record by making 67 three-pointers. Although Santa Clara was just a mediocre team, Nash was named an All-WCC guard and emerged as one of the top point guards in the nation.

Nash also became the Broncos' best player and leader. Nobody on the team worked harder than him. He would dribble a tennis ball around campus to hone his dribbling skills. He dragged teammates out of their dorm rooms to play pick-up games late at night. He once even practiced his shot in a heavy rainstorm on Christmas Eve.

"Every sprint that we run, he wins," said Davey, who became Santa Clara's head coach when Nash arrived. "Every drill, he tries to be first. He has such deep, competitive desire."[2]

"Steve is really deranged," Davey added. "He's addicted to basketball, and fortunately he's helped derange the whole team."[3]

SHOWING HIS POTENTIAL

In 1994, during the summer after his sophomore year, Nash made the Canadian international team and played in the World Championship of Basketball. The Canadians were overmatched by most teams, but Nash made a strong impression on observers. After watching him play, Del Harris, an advisor to the

Canadian team and a former NBA head coach, told Nash that he would soon be an NBA player.

In one memorable exhibition against Spain that summer, Nash played the entire game. He scored 32 points, had 12 assists, and pulled down 10 rebounds.

"That's when you knew he probably had what it takes" to play in the NBA, recalled Mike Katz, who coached the Canadian team.[4]

Nash returned to Santa Clara for his junior season ready for a breakout. That is exactly what happened. He led the WCC in scoring with 20.9 points per game and assists with 6.4. The Broncos won their first regular season WCC title since 1970. Although they lost in the WCC Tournament, the Broncos were awarded an at-large berth in the 1995 NCAA Tournament.

They were seeded No. 12 in the West region and faced No. 5 seed Mississippi State in the first round. Nash scored 22 points and dished out 6 assists as the Broncos hung with the Bulldogs, but eventually fell 75–67.

SANTA CLARA'S RECORDS WITH NASH

1992–93: 19–12, 9–5 in WCC (3rd), won WCC Tournament.

1993–94: 13–14, 6–8 in WCC (Tie-5th), lost in first round of WCC Tournament.

1994–95: 21–7, 12–2 in WCC (1st), lost in first round of WCC Tournament.

1995–96: 20–9, 10–4 in WCC (Tie-1st), lost in first round of WCC Tournament.

CHOOSING COLLEGE

After the season, Nash was named the WCC Player of the Year. NBA scouts were raving about his talent, and experts predicted that, if he declared for the NBA Draft, he would be a first-round pick.

But Nash was not finished at Santa Clara. He liked his teammates too much and loved playing college basketball. He also knew he could improve his game. So he returned for his senior season.

Nash prepared for that season by continuing to train and playing pickup games with NBA players such as Brian Shaw and Jason Kidd.

His decision to stay in college paid dividends. With such a high-profile player as Nash, the Broncos were scheduled to play on national television early in the 1995–96 season for the first time in school history. They took advantage of their exposure. They beat UCLA, the defending national champion, 78–69, on ESPN in the opening game of November's Maui Invitational.

The Broncos later defeated big-time programs Oregon State, Georgia Tech, and Michigan State, as well. They went 10–4 in WCC play and won a share of a second straight conference title.

SANTA CLARA IN THE NCAA TOURNAMENT WITH NASH

1993: Beat Arizona 64–61 in first round. Lost to Temple 68–57 in second round.

1995: Lost to Mississippi State 75–67 in first round.

1996: Beat Maryland 91–79 in first round. Lost to Kansas 76–51 in second round.

Nash was named WCC Player of the Year again. He led the conference with a free-throw shooting percentage of .894. Some experts called him the best point guard in the country.

"He may be the most solid of the bunch," *Sports Illustrated* said in an early season story about Nash. "Kansas' Jacque Vaughn may direct traffic better, but his outside shot isn't as good as Nash's. Georgetown's Allen Iverson is a terrific talent but still turns the ball over too much and makes a lower percentage of his shots than Nash does."[5]

Santa Clara lost in the WCC Tournament but was again awarded an at-large NCAA Tournament berth. The Broncos were a No. 10 seed and faced No. 7 seed Maryland in the first round of the West region, in Tempe, Arizona, on March 15, 1996.

Nash dominated the Terrapins, often breaking their full-court press and passing to his teammates for open baskets. He finished with 12 assists and 28 points, making 17 of 18 free throws, as the Broncos knocked off Maryland 91–79.

Nash's collegiate career came to an end two days later when the No. 2-seeded Kansas Jayhawks beat Santa Clara 76–51 in the second round. With future NBA players such as Paul Pierce, Raef LaFrentz, and Vaughn, Kansas was too loaded for the Broncos to handle. Vaughn helped hold Nash to 7 points in a matchup of two of the nation's best point guards.

NASH'S SANTA CLARA STATS

(All but steals are per-game averages)

1992–93: 8.1 points, 2.2 assists, 2.6 rebounds, 26 steals

1993–94: 14.6 points, 3.7 assists, 2.5 rebounds, 34 steals

1994–95: 20.9 points, 6.4 assists, 3.8 rebounds, 48 steals

1995–96: 17 points, 6.0 assists, 3.6 rebounds, 39 steals

Career: 14.9 points, 4.5 assists, 3.1 rebounds, 147 steals

Still, as Nash prepared for the upcoming NBA Draft, he was content with how his Santa Clara career had unfolded.

Three months later, Nash was chosen by the Phoenix Suns in the first round of the NBA Draft. He had achieved his childhood goal, but he would quickly find out that playing in the NBA would be much more difficult than playing college basketball.

STEVE NASH IN THE SANTA CLARA RECORD BOOKS

Most three-pointers in a game, 8, vs. Gonzaga, January 19, 1995 (tied with Mitch Burley, 1988)

Most three-pointers in a season, 84, in 1994–95

Most three-pointers in a career, 263

Most free throws made in a game, 21, vs. St. Mary's, January 7, 1995

Most assists in a game, 15, vs. Southern, December 9, 1995

Best career three-point shooting percentage, .401

Best career free-throw shooting percentage, .867

Fourth in career points, with 1,689

Second in career assists, 510

CHAPTER FOUR

Competing for Playing Time

On June 26, 1996, NBA commissioner David Stern walked to a podium inside the Meadowlands Complex in East Rutherford, New Jersey. He announced that the Phoenix Suns had selected Steve Nash with the 15th pick of the NBA Draft.

Nash was only the second former Canadian high school player to be picked in the first round of an NBA Draft. He was the third point guard chosen in 1996, after Allen Iverson and Stephon Marbury.

"We think Steve is a terrific player," Suns' assistant coach Danny Ainge said. "We like the way he enters the ball in the post. We like the way he runs the floor. We like the way he can shoot, and we're very excited to have him."[1]

A ROUGH START

Some experts tabbed Nash as the best pure point guard in the draft. Many people did not agree—including fans of the Suns. When the Suns' pick was announced inside Phoenix's AmericaWest Arena, the Suns' home court, a few thousand Suns fans who had gathered there to watch the draft booed.

Nash gave them little reason to cheer once his rookie season started a few months later. The Suns' plan was for him to come off the bench and give breaks to starting point guard Kevin Johnson. Club officials thought Nash could learn a lot from Johnson, who was in his ninth full season with Phoenix. They expected Nash to replace Johnson in the starting lineup the next season when Johnson retired.

That plan never materialized.

The Suns got off to a terrible start. They were a team in transition, a few months removed from trading away franchise cornerstone Charles Barkley. They lost

POINT GUARDS CHOSEN IN THE 1996 NBA DRAFT

Allen Iverson
(No. 1, Philadelphia 76ers)

Stephon Marbury
(No. 4, Milwaukee Bucks, traded to Minnesota Timberwolves on Draft Day)

Steve Nash
(No. 15, Phoenix Suns)

Tony Delk
(No. 16, Charlotte Hornets)

Derek Fisher
(No. 24, Los Angeles Lakers)

Moochie Norris
(No. 33, Milwaukee Bucks)

Jeff McInnis
(No. 37, Denver Nuggets)

Randy Livingston
(No. 42, Houston Rockets)

Reggie Geary
(No. 56, Cleveland Cavaliers)

Shawn Harvey
(No. 34, Dallas Mavericks)

Drew Barry
(No. 57, Seattle SuperSonics)

Nash reacts to being chosen by the Suns in the NBA Draft.

their first thirteen games of the season and were so disorganized that head coach Cotton Fitzsimmons decided to retire.

A GOOD CHANGE

Then Ainge took over. Ainge knew basketball. He had a distinguished NBA career as a player. He was a starting guard on two Boston Celtics teams that won NBA championships in the 1980s. He had played for Suns and Portland Trail Blazers teams that advanced to the NBA Finals in the early 1990s.

Most important for Nash, Ainge loved point guards and was not afraid to try unconventional things. Those traits would boost Nash after the Suns made a trade that could have been devastating to his career.

THE CHARLES BARKLEY TRADE OF 1996

On August 19, 1996, two months after they drafted Steve Nash, the Suns traded Charles Barkley and a second-round draft pick to the Houston Rockets for Sam Cassell, Robert Horry, Chucky Brown, and Mark Bryant.

Midway through the 1996–97 season, the Suns began to pull themselves out of their early tailspin. They had Johnson, Nash, and several other talented offensive players, such as Wesley Person, Rex Chapman, Sam Cassell, and second-year player Michael Finley.

On December 26, 1996, they again decided to make a major overhaul of their team. The Suns traded Finley and Cassell, among others, to the Mavericks for standout point guard Jason Kidd. The trade meant that the Suns now had three point guards capable of playing a lot of minutes. It would be difficult to find enough playing time to satisfy each of them.

Ainge did what he thought was best for the team. He played all three of them. Kidd started and played most of the game. Johnson shifted often to shooting guard. Nash saw time off the bench at both positions. Ainge's strategy was for the Suns to play "small ball," relying on their wealth of guards to outscore opponents.

It worked. The Suns pulled together and finished 40–42, not bad considering their awful start. They made the NBA Playoffs, getting the No. 7 seed in the Western Conference. In the first round, they pushed the second-seeded Seattle SuperSonics to the brink of elimination before falling in five games.

THE DECEMBER 26, 1996, TRADE

The Suns traded Sam Cassell, Michael Finley, A.C. Green, and a draft pick to the Dallas Mavericks for Jason Kidd, Tony Dumas, and Loren Meyer.

PHOENIX SUNS VS. SEATTLE SUPERSONICS, 1997 NBA PLAYOFFS FIRST ROUND

Game 1: Suns 106, Sonics 101

Game 2: Sonics 122, Suns 78

Game 3: Suns 110, Sonics 103

Game 4: Sonics 122, Suns 115, overtime

Game 5: Sonics 116, Suns 92

Nash had a decent rookie season. Because he was playing behind Kidd and Johnson, he played only about 10 minutes per game. He did average 2 assists per game, projecting to nearly 10 assists in a full game.

He scored 17 points and had 12 assists and 7 rebounds in his only start of the season, on November 14, 1996, in Vancouver. But he was far from satisfied with how the season went.

"My main concern was how I'm going to make myself better, so I can be successful—regardless of who's here," Nash said.

> **"My main concern was how I'm going to make myself better."**
>
> **—Steve Nash**

"I probably didn't deserve a lot of minutes, no matter how ready or how good I was," Nash added. "We had two All-Star point guards. I understood."[2]

But he should have played more minutes, according to Ainge. Recognizing Nash's abilities, Ainge played Nash much more in his second season. Despite playing on a team that had Kidd, Johnson, Chapman, and Dennis Scott in the

THE PHOENIX SUNS' POINT GUARDS, 1997–98

(ALL ARE PER-GAME AVERAGES, EXCEPT STARTS)

- Jason Kidd: 11.6 points, 9.1 assists, 6.2 rebounds, 38.0 minutes, 82 starts
- Kevin Johnson: 9.5 points, 4.9 assists, 3.3 rebounds, 25.8 minutes, 12 starts
- Steve Nash: 9.1 points, 3.4 assists, 2.1 rebounds, 21.9 minutes, 9 starts

backcourt, Nash earned more than 21 minutes per game. He averaged more than 9 points and 3 assists and helped the Suns have an excellent season.

"My attitude has always been to learn, excel and expand my game," Nash said. "Most people told me, 'You'll never play with those two guys [Kidd and Johnson] there.' But now that I've worked my way into that position, I want to keep growing. The coaches will have to get me into more games."[3]

During one six-game stretch in January, Nash shot better than 60 percent from three-point range and averaged 13.5 points per game in almost 27 minutes of action per game.

"He's better than half the starting point guards in the league right now," Ainge said during that outburst. "I love the guy."[4]

EARNING MORE PLAYING TIME

Nash made an impact on offense because of his shooting, but he also became a decent NBA defender that season. That development helped him earn minutes.

"Even though I'm shooting the ball well and scoring," Nash said in mid-season, "the key is still my defensive energy and intensity and the problems I give to other teams' guards."[5]

Phoenix went 56–26 and finished third in the Pacific Division, behind the Lakers and Sonics. The Suns' small ball style helped them run past many teams. Their three point guards moved the ball around like a pinball game. Along with Kidd and Johnson, Nash helped the Suns lead the NBA in team assists per game with 25.9.

Phoenix suffered an injury to Danny Manning, one of its few big men, late in the season. Without Manning, the Suns could not contain big men David Robinson and Tim Duncan in the playoffs and fell to the San Antonio Spurs in the first round.

PHOENIX SUNS VS. SAN ANTONIO SPURS, 1998 NBA PLAYOFFS FIRST ROUND

Game 1: Spurs 102, Suns 96

Game 2: Suns 108, Spurs 101

Game 3: Spurs 100, Suns 88

Game 4: Spurs 99, Suns 80

Ainge came to count on Nash as the season unfolded, especially when Kidd and Johnson missed games due to injury. Despite his increased minutes and the team's success, Nash wanted to play more.

"It was tough," he said. "But you can't worry about things you have no control over. I just wanted to be ready when my opportunity came."[6]

A NEW TEAM

Nash would get that opportunity after the season. With Kidd firmly entrenched as their point guard and desperate for help in the frontcourt, the Suns made another trade with the Mavericks after the 1997–98 season. This time they sent Nash to Dallas.

Nash arrived in the summer of 1998 with high expectations and a great opportunity. The Mavericks were making him their starting point guard. He was excited about the change and confident about his chances for success in Dallas. After all, he had learned how to run an NBA team from two masters.

"What I take most from KJ [Johnson] is his confidence in his ability to take over games by scoring and penetrating," Nash said shortly after the trade. "Jason [Kidd] is so confident and plays so hard. He affects the game on so many levels and causes a lot of doubt in other teams' minds."[7]

Unfortunately for Nash, there was doubt in other minds as well—the minds of Dallas Mavericks fans. Few of them believed Nash was the man who could turn their lousy team around. He would just have to prove another group of people wrong.

CHAPTER FIVE

Struggling as a Maverick

After his strong play during the 1997–98 season, Nash was a hot commodity in the NBA. His rookie contract was scheduled to expire after the next season, and the Phoenix Suns already had Jason Kidd set as their point guard. NBA general managers knew the Suns probably would have to trade Nash after the season.

Several teams made offers for Nash, and the Suns eventually struck a deal with the Dallas Mavericks. On June 25, 1998, Dallas sent two role players, a rookie, and a 1999 first-round pick to Phoenix for Nash. Later that week, the Mavericks introduced Nash along with new teammate Dirk Nowitzki, a tall twenty-year-old German whom they acquired in another trade on the night of the 1998 NBA Draft.

CAPTAIN NASH

The Mavs immediately named Nash a team co-captain. "He's the point guard. It's his team," said head coach Don Nelson. "He doesn't have to win a job in training camp."[1]

That was music to Nash's ears. Nelson also announced that he had signed Nash to a contract extension. Nash and Nowitzki, Nelson said, would team with forward Michael Finley to form the nucleus of Dallas' teams for years to come.

THE JUNE 25, 1998, TRADE

The Phoenix Suns sent Steve Nash to Dallas for Martin Muursepp, Bubba Wells, Pat Garrity, and Dallas' 1999 first-round pick, Shawn Marion.

"The future is in their hands," Nelson said, adding that Nash and Finley would be "captains for as long as I'm going to be here."[2]

Many fans and experts scoffed at Nelson's plan. It was just another misguided attempt to turn around the club, they thought. The Mavericks were nicknamed the "Mav-wrecks" by fans because they had

THE DON NELSON FILE

Three-time NBA Coach of the Year: 1983, 1985, 1992

Head coach for Milwaukee Bucks (1976–87), Golden State Warriors (1987–95), New York Knicks (1995–96), and Dallas Mavericks (1997–2005)

All-time record: 1,190–880; guided Dallas and Milwaukee to the conference finals

Steve Nash dribbles past Tyronn Lue of the Los Angeles Lakers in a game on November 7, 1999.

experienced nearly a decade of losing, including a 20–62 record in 1997–98. They had not qualified for the playoffs since the 1989–90 season. Since then, they had introduced many new players and said they were the ones who would make Dallas a winner.

Nash, Nowitzki, and Finley hardly seemed to be any different than those busts. Finley was the leading scorer on the 1997–98 Mavs. However, he was considered to be at best the No. 2 or No. 3 option on a good team—not the go-to guy. Plus, those 1997–98 Mavs were terrible.

THE MAVERICKS' WOES

Ten straight seasons out of the playoffs (1990–91 through 1999–2000)

Ten straight losing seasons (1990–91 through 1999–2000)

11–71 record in 1992–93

Nicknamed "Mav-wrecks" by fans

Nowitzki was an unknown, an example of a new trend in the NBA. Many teams were drafting young, tall European players with shooting skills and seemingly unlimited potential. Unfortunately for the Mavs, many of the European players to that point had failed to reach their potential.

Trading for Nowitzki especially angered Mavs fans. The Mavs could have selected Kansas forward Paul Pierce or St. Louis guard Larry Hughes, both American college stars, in the draft. Instead they picked Michigan forward

THE MICHAEL FINLEY FILE

Born March 6, 1973, and grew up in Chicago

6' 7", 225 pounds

College: Wisconsin

Drafted by the Phoenix Suns in the first round (No. 21 overall) of 1995 NBA Draft. Traded by the Suns to the Mavericks on December 26, 1996.

Started all 82 games, averaging 21.5 points for Dallas in 1997–98.

1998–99 and 1999–2000 average with Steve Nash in Dallas: 21.6 points and 5.9 rebounds.

THE DIRK NOWITZKI FILE

Born June 19, 1978, in Germany.

7-feet tall, 245 pounds

Drafted by the Milwaukee Bucks in the first round (No. 9 overall) of 1998 NBA Draft. Traded to Mavericks with Pat Garrity for Robert Traylor on draft night, June 24, 1998.

1998–99 and 1999–2000 average with Steve Nash in Dallas: 14.1 points and 5.4 rebounds per game.

THE 1998 NBA DRAFT

1. Michael Olowakandi (Los Angeles Clippers)

2. Mike Bibby (Vancouver Grizzlies)

3. Raef LaFrentz (Denver Nuggets)

4. Antwan Jamison (Toronto Raptors)

5. Vince Carter (Golden State Warriors)

6. Robert Traylor (Dallas Mavericks)

7. Jason Williams (Sacramento Kings)

8. Larry Hughes (Philadelphia 76ers)

9. Dirk Nowitzki (Milwaukee Bucks)

10. Paul Pierce (Boston Celtics)

Robert Traylor, then traded him to Milwaukee for Nowitzki, who was the ninth pick. The Mavs also got Pat Garrity but shipped him to Phoenix in the deal for Nash.

Nash, despite his growth in Phoenix, was still doubted by many basketball fans and insiders because of his small size and limited experience. In two NBA seasons, he had started only 11 games and rarely played at the end of close games. Yet Nelson awarded him a six-year, $33 million contract and handed him the keys to the Mavs.

A SEASON CUT SHORT

Nash relished the chance to prove the critics wrong. But the 1998–99 season, his first in Dallas, would prove to be maybe the most difficult one of his career.

Before the Mavs could even get started, training camp and exhibitions were cancelled when the NBA locked out players because of a labor dispute. The league and the NBA Players' Union could not agree on how to share revenue, how long rookie contracts should be, and how to set other business regulations. The two parties failed to make compromises at several meetings, and the lockout lasted six months.

By the time the parties signed an agreement, it was January, two months after the regular season usually started. The NBA drew up a new shortened schedule, and teams underwent brief training camps, playing only a few exhibitions before the regular season began.

With two new players in key roles, the Mavs were hurt as much as any team by the lockout. They struggled to build team chemistry. Nowitzki was nervous about coming to play in the United States for the first time and never got comfortable. Nash struggled with injuries and with running a team for the first time.

THE NBA LOCKOUT

The NBA lockout lasted from July 1, 1998, to January 6, 1999. It forced the NBA to cancel 32 games for each team, shortening the regular season to 50 games.

The result was the Mavs flopped. Dallas went 19–31, one of the worst records in the NBA. Nash missed ten games with injuries and played others with a painful stress fracture in his back. He averaged 7.9

points and 5.5 assists in the 40 games he played. He averaged about 32 minutes of playing time per game, a low figure for a starter, especially a point guard.

"I was pressing, I didn't really fit in yet, I didn't react to a new situation well, and I wasn't real fit, health-wise," Nash said. "But the bottom line is I didn't play my game."[3]

"Steve is basically a capsule of our entire team," assistant coach Don Nelson said. "Individually, we have to step it up as a team, and we also have to gel together."[4]

Nash was so inconsistent that, during a long losing streak, Mavs fans booed him in a March 24 game against the Houston Rockets. Nash did not mind the booing. He showed he could handle the pressure of being the starting point guard with the big contract.

"My little brother, Martin, was at the game, and I looked up at him and he was laughing his butt off," Nash recalled. "I just started laughing. I knew right then, how can you let something so silly and so meaningless in life affect you?"[5]

"Whether the fans like me or not is totally irrelevant at this point," Nash added. "My number one concern is the team. The fans have to be secondary. If the fans have given up on me, that's fine."[6]

Luckily, the fans had not given up. One of the few bright spots for the Mavs in the lockout-shortened season was their performance at home. They went

15–10, sparking the development of a home-court advantage that would be key in future seasons.

There were other silver linings for the Mavs during the 1998–99 season. Finley played in all 50 games, extending his streak of consecutive games played to nearly 300. He also averaged more than 20 points per game and was the 12th highest-scoring player in the NBA.

GOOD CHEMISTRY

Nash and Nowitzki, meanwhile, became close friends. They would often go to the Mavs' practice gym at night to play one-on-one games. Nowitzki moved

Mavericks forward Dirk Nowitzki gets a pat on the head from teammate Steve Nash.

into an apartment in the same building as Nash, who became his mentor. Nash was like an older brother to him. Nowitzki was glad to have Nash on his team.

"Steve's such a nice guy, so we got along great right from the beginning," Nowitzki said. "I would've felt really alone here if it wasn't for him."[7]

"You've got to believe their friendship was born out of the controversy surrounding them when they first came here," Don Nelson said. "To go through the grinder like Steve and Dirk did, to be booed on your own court, to be called every name in the book and have your name dragged in the mud? How can two people not bond together when they were both under a microscope?"[8]

Finley's consistency and the developing chemistry between Nowitzki and Nash gave the Mavs hope heading into the next season. Nash knew he was expected to produce a lot more than he had in his first season in Dallas, especially after the team was criticized in the off-season.

Nelson, for example, defended Nash before the 1999 NBA Draft. Dallas did not have a first-round pick because Nelson had dealt it as part of the trade for Nash a year earlier.

> "Steve's such a nice guy, so we got along great right from the beginning."
>
> —Dirk Nowitzki

"We thought Nash would be better than any pick we could get, and I still believe that," Nelson said. "Now he has to become the player I know he is."[9]

That would take a little while. The 1999–2000 season began without any hint of a breakthrough. Early on, the Mavs again fell way below .500 and out of playoff contention. Nash struggled with injuries and his confidence. Nowitzki still had trouble adapting to the American game.

Nash drives to the basket against the Raptors in 2000.

AN IMPORTANT ARGUMENT

The Mavs seemed destined for a tenth straight losing season when they suddenly encountered two big turning points. First, owner Ross Perot Jr. sold the team to Mark Cuban, a young billionaire who pledged to spend as much money on

> # "It wasn't an easy meeting."
>
> ## –Don Nelson

the Mavs as he needed to make them contenders again. Then Nash and Nelson had a critical argument.

Nelson said that throughout most of Nash's first two seasons in Dallas, he hesitated to shoot the ball. He was too concerned with getting teammates involved and was not scoring enough points to help the team win. The Mavs needed to take advantage of Nash's excellent shooting skills in order to be a better team.

At first, Nash did not agree with Nelson. On March 9, 2000, the Mavs were in the midst of another tailspin. Nelson confronted Nash in the weight room of Dallas' Reunion Arena, where the Mavs trained. The two got into a heated argument. When they were finished, Nash understood Nelson's perspective and agreed to start shooting more.

"It wasn't an easy meeting, it wasn't a fun meeting," Nelson said. "There wasn't a lack of effort on his part, it was just his mentality. Here's a guy who's got a gift shooting the basketball, and I told him that by not using it, he was taking away one-third of his skills."[10]

"Nellie got on me and wanted more from me," Nash said. "And I just wanted more of an opportunity from him. I think it kind of cleared the air and allowed us to move forward. Things really went up from there."[11]

The results were clear almost immediately. Nash increased his scoring average, and the Mavs became a dangerous team. They won 30 of their final 48 games, including a 9–1 record to close the season in April.

Nash increased his scoring average slightly from the previous year, averaging 8.6 points for the season. He missed twenty-six games and did not start in twenty-nine others, when Nelson benched him for a while in mid-season. Once Nash returned to the starting lineup healthy at the end of the year, the Mavs were much improved.

With Nash shooting more, opponents had to respect his jump shot, creating more open space for Finley and Nowitzki to work on offense. Both took advantage. Finley averaged a career high in scoring and was named an All-Star for the first time. Nowitzki more than doubled his scoring average compared to his rookie year.

DID YOU KNOW?

Michael Finley played in 490 consecutive games, dating from his rookie season (1995–96) to December 29, 2001. He did not miss a single game in any of his first five seasons in Dallas.

Finally, it appeared the Mavs had been rebuilt and were on the verge of becoming a winning team.

CHAPTER SIX

An Olympic Turnaround

After his hot finish to the 1999–2000 season, Nash was healthy and confident in the summer of 2000. The twenty-six-year-old was looking forward to returning to Dallas in the fall to see what he, Finley, Nowitzki, and the rest of the Mavs could accomplish.

Before the season began, though, Nash had another challenge in front of him.

REPRESENTING HIS COUNTRY

Team Canada had qualified for the Summer Olympics, and Nash would be the starting point guard for the Games in Sydney, Australia. It was a big honor for Nash, who loved playing for his home country.

Nash celebrates Canada's upset victory against Yugoslavia during the Olympics in Sydney, Australia, September 25, 2000.

The Canadians were huge underdogs in the tournament. The American team had a dozen NBA All-Stars, while the European teams also had several NBA players. Other than Nash, the only NBA player on Canada's roster was center Todd MacCulloch.

Nash could have sat out the Olympics, as a few Canadian-born NBA players did. He could have used the rest to prepare for the upcoming NBA season, but he insisted on playing. He was named the captain of the Canadian team. He immediately became its leader and worked hard to prepare for the September Games.

Nash took his role as team captain very seriously. Because most of his teammates were not NBA players, they could not afford to spend much money or enjoy Sydney when they were not playing. So Nash gave coach Jay Triano $25,000 for spending cash to distribute among his teammates. That generosity and his personality helped Nash fit right in with his teammates.

"He just hangs out with the guys," said teammate Shawn Swords. "He doesn't try to be a prima donna. He rides in coach [on planes] with the rest of us. He doesn't ask for his own [hotel] room. He's a good guy. It has nothing to do with the money or his basketball skills. If he wasn't a basketball player, he'd be my friend."[1]

Nash's leadership helped Canada stage a historic run during the 12-team Olympic tournament. The Canadians went 4–1 during preliminary round-robin play. They finished atop Group B in a tie with Yugoslavia and clinched a berth in the eight-team single-elimination round.

The Canadians beat the host Australians. Nash scored 15 points and dished out 15 assists. The Canadians shocked the heavily favored Yugoslavians. In that game Nash poured in 26 points and had

GROUP B STANDINGS
(PRELIMINARY ROUND)

1. Canada 4–1

2. Yugoslavia 4–1

3. Australia 3–2

4. Russia 3–2

5. Spain 1–4

6. Angola 0–5

8 assists and 8 rebounds. He either scored or assisted on 18 of Canada's final 21 points as it iced the game down the stretch.

"Steve had that look before the game," said Canada coach Jay Triano. "He just looked at me and smiled. I said, 'You should smile. This is the Olympics.'"[2]

"I wish everyone had the chance to be part of a group like this at some point in their lives."

—Steve Nash

Although Canada lost to France in the quarterfinals, Nash and his teammates bounced back two days later. Nash scored 14 points and handed out 3 assists to lead the Canadians past Russia, 86–83 in double overtime, in the seventh-place game.

In seven games overall during the tournament, Nash led Team Canada in scoring, assists, and rebounds.

"I'm really proud to be a part of this team," he said after their final game. "I wish everyone had the chance to be part of a group like this at some point in their lives."[3]

2000 SUMMER OLYMPICS MEN'S BASKETBALL STANDINGS

1. United States
2. France
3. Lithuania
4. Australia
5. Italy
6. Yugoslavia
7. Canada
8. Russia

A SHOT OF CONFIDENCE

Nash's stellar play and leadership in the Olympics marked a defining moment in his career. That boosted him as he returned to the United States for NBA training camp just days after the Olympics ended. He carried with him a bruised knee and a reinjured back, injuries he suffered during the Olympics. But those setbacks would not halt his momentum.

"Sometimes it takes an experience that has nothing to do with the NBA to kick-start a player," said Doc Rivers, then the Orlando Magic head coach. "Steve Nash always had it in him, but he needed that confidence boost [from the Olympics] . . . . It was crucial."[4]

2000–01 NBA MIDWEST DIVISION STANDINGS
1. San Antonio Spurs 58–24
2. Utah Jazz 53–29
3. Dallas Mavericks 53–29
4. Minnesota Timberwolves 47–35
5. Houston Rockets 45–37
6. Denver Nuggets 40–42
7. Vancouver Grizzlies 23–59

The Mavericks capitalized on Nash's renewed confidence, picking up right where they had left off at the end of the 1999–2000 season. The 2000–01 campaign would prove to be the breakout season for which the franchise and its fans had waited. The Mavs won more than 50 games. They finished tied for second in the Midwest Division and fifth in the tough Western Conference.

Nash averaged a career-high 15.6 points, nearly doubling his average of a year earlier. He also dished out a career-high 7.9 assists per game. He missed twelve games due to injury but started in all seventy games that he played.

On one memorable January night, Nash set a new career high by scoring 27 points during a win in Toronto. He was given a standing ovation before the game by the Canadian crowd, which was still thrilled with his play in the Olympics.

Nash was asked to score more for the Canadians than he had for the Mavs. When he met that challenge in Sydney, he returned to Dallas a more aggressive, confident player.

"I think the Olympic experience really helped me, the way [Team Canada] counted on me," Nash said. "It's not my nature to be that aggressive. I'd rather get the ball to my teammates, but that team needed me to score.

"Now, when this team [the Mavs] has asked me to score, it's made the transition easier for me."[5]

Taking on more of the scoring load also helped Nash assert himself as a Maverick. He became an unquestioned leader, justifying his co-captaincy. He picked up some of the slack that Finley had been carrying for years.

"It's been so much easier for me this year," Finley said. "Now the pressure isn't all on me. I finally have some help."[6]

Nash really showed his importance to the Mavs during the Western Conference Playoffs. The Mavs qualified for the playoffs for the first time in eleven years. Dallas was seeded fifth and played the No. 4 seed, the Utah Jazz, in the opening round.

AN UNDERDOG AGAIN

The Jazz still had forward Karl Malone and guard John Stockton, both All-Stars, plus other key players who had helped them get to consecutive NBA Finals in 1997 and 1998. They were heavily favored against the Mavs.

The series unfolded just as the experts had predicted in the first two games. Playing in front of one of the loudest home crowds in the NBA, the Jazz edged the Mavs 88–86 in Game 1 and beat them again in Game 2, 109–98.

Nash played decently in the first two playoff games of his career, scoring 20 points apiece in games 1 and 2. But the Mavs blew a six-point lead in the final five minutes of Game 1, and Nash missed a key three-point attempt that would have tied Game 2 in the fourth quarter. The Jazz then quickly blew that game open.

The series began to turn around after it moved to Dallas for Game 3. In the best-of-five-series, the Mavs needed to win Game 3 in order to avoid elimination.

Midway through the third quarter, Nash and Stockton collided. Stockton banged his front teeth on Nash's forehead. Nash was bleeding badly and had to

Utah Jazz guard John Stockton pressures Dallas' Steve Nash during a 2001 game in Salt Lake City.

leave the game. He appeared to be done for the night, which would be a crushing blow to the Mavs' hopes.

Instead, the Mavs trainers used seven stitches to close the deep cut on Nash's forehead, and he re-entered the game. Then, with the Mavs trailing 91–90 in the final minute, Nash put the game in his own hands when his team got the ball back.

With Stockton draped all over him, Nash launched a 12-foot turnaround jumper over Stockton. The ball dropped through the basket with 22 seconds left. Nash's shot gave Dallas a 92–91 edge. The Jazz could not respond, and the Mavs held on for their first win of the series, 94–91. It was the franchise's first playoff win in more than a decade.

"I just knew we needed to counter," Nash said of taking the crucial shot. "We didn't have much time. I knew we needed to make a shot."[7]

Nash was thrilled to get the better of Stockton. He considered Stockton to be one of the three best point guards of all time and a personal role model. Nash's play earned praise from his coach.

"Steve has done a great job of hanging in there," Nelson said after the game. "I don't think you would say he is better than John Stockton, but he sure is battling him."[8]

Three days later, the Mavs blasted Utah 107–77 in Game 4. Nash outscored Stockton 27–4, making 4-of-8 three-pointers, as the Mavs tied the series at two games apiece.

The series returned to Salt Lake City for the fifth and decisive game. That was the same city where Nash had first

"Steve has done a great job of hanging in there."

—Coach Nelson

emerged on the national basketball stage, making the clutch free throws as a Santa Clara freshman against Arizona in the 1993 NCAA Tournament.

At first, the Jazz dominated Game 5, and Nash struggled. Utah opened up a 17-point lead in the third quarter and still held a big lead in the fourth. Nash did not score a single point in the first three quarters. He also hurt his ankle when Jazz center Greg Ostertag landed on it.

Then Nash got hot. He made a three-pointer to cut Utah's lead to nine points. He made another three-pointer and then hit his third of the quarter to tie the game, 79–79, with about four minutes to play.

Nash's teammates picked up the slack from there. Center Calvin Booth made a short bank shot with less than 10 seconds to play to complete an 84–83 victory against the Jazz. Utah's fans inside the Delta Center—and basketball experts and fans everywhere—were stunned.

Nash finished with 9 points and 7 assists in the game. They were not great numbers, but he did not care. "Tonight, our perseverance was the key," Nash said.

"This is right there with the Olympics, Santa Clara, everything," he added.

2001 NBA PLAYOFFS DALLAS MAVERICKS VS. UTAH JAZZ FIRST-ROUND SERIES

Game 1: Jazz 88, Mavericks 86

Game 2: Jazz 109, Mavericks 98

Game 3: Mavericks 94, Jazz 91

Game 4: Mavericks 107, Jazz 77

Game 5: Mavericks 84, Jazz 83

TEAMS TO RALLY FROM A 0-2 DEFICIT IN A BEST-OF-FIVE NBA FIRST-ROUND PLAYOFF SERIES

Dallas Mavericks
(2001 against Utah Jazz)
Denver Nuggets
(1994 against Seattle
SuperSonics)
Phoenix Suns
(1993 against Los Angeles
Lakers)
New York Knicks
(1990 against Boston Celtics)
Golden State Warriors
(1987 against Jazz)

"From Game 1 to now, I think you have to say that we did just enough to win."[9]

The Mavs did what few people thought was possible. Not only did they make the playoffs and win more than 50 regular season games, they knocked off a veteran team in the first round of the playoffs without home-court advantage. They also became just the fifth team in NBA history to rally from a 2–0 deficit to win a best-of-five NBA first-round playoff series.

"It's unbelievable," said Mavs owner Mark Cuban. "I'm just sitting here trying to take a mental video and savor all of this."[10]

Next up were the San Antonio Spurs, the No. 1 seed in the West. The Spurs had won the NBA title only two years earlier and had two of the best big men in the game, Tim Duncan and David Robinson.

It would be tough for the Mavs to beat another playoff-tested team. In fact, they could not. San Antonio won the first three games, including Game 3 in Dallas. Yet the Mavs would not wilt. In Game 4,

Nash scored 10 points and had 14 assists, while Nowitzki scored 30, as the Mavs won 112–108. But the Spurs won Game 5 at home to clinch the series.

Although they lost to the Spurs, 4–1, the Mavs were proud of what they had accomplished in

2000–01. Now they were eager to take the next step and become an NBA title contender. They knew that would be much harder than going from perennial loser to a winning team.

As long as the Mavs had Nash around, they were confident they could do it. Nash had come out of his funk, emerging as one of the best point guards in the game.

"That kick in the teeth he got here when he was

booed by our home fans [early in his Dallas career], it bothered him more than he'll admit," Nelson said. "It took him longer to come out of it than I anticipated, but when he came out of it, he was a stronger man for it. I don't know where we'd be without him."[11]

CHAPTER SEVEN

A Team Proving Itself

The Mavs entered the 2001–02 season with high hopes and a new standard. No longer would it be considered a triumph to just make the playoffs. After winning 54 regular season games and beating the Jazz in the first round of the 2001 NBA Playoffs, the Mavs expected to become one of the NBA's elite teams and contend for a championship.

That would be easier said than done. With its nucleus of Steve Nash, Dirk Nowitzki, and Michael Finley, the Mavs were one of the highest scoring teams in the league. But Dallas had a big weakness. Simply put, the Mavs did not play good defense.

That weakness would come to haunt them in 2001–02.

A STELLAR SEASON

The Mavs tore through the regular season. Dallas won 57 games, finishing second in the Midwest Division and fourth in the Western Conference. They set a new franchise record for victories and road wins in a season.

Nash had another great season. He averaged a career high 17.9 points and 7.7 assists, playing in all 82 games for the first time in his career. He set a new single-game career high by scoring 39 points in a game against the Portland Trail Blazers. He was named an All-Star for the first time in his career, becoming the first Canadian in NBA history to earn that honor.

Nash was a big reason why the Mavs set an NBA record for fewest turnovers in an 82-game season. He had become so consistent and effective that he was regarded as one of the best point guards in the game.

"He is the heart and soul of the Mavericks," said Alvin Gentry, the coach of the Los Angeles Clippers at that time. "They never lose if he plays well or has a huge game."[1]

The Mavs geared up for a playoff run by making a move. They acquired spunky point guard Nick Van Exel,

DID YOU KNOW?
The Mavs led the NBA in scoring with 105.2 points per game in 2001–02 but were 28th out of 29 teams in points allowed at 101. The Mavs were second in the NBA in shooting percentage with an average of .507.

among others, in a trade with the Denver Nuggets. Van Exel had developed a reputation as somebody who took too many shots and did not get along well with his teammates. But in the Mavs offense he fit just fine, despite often playing with Nash, another point guard.

"This offense is a point guard's offense, and Steve should really flourish in it," Van Exel said. "He is made for it, with the way he plays, always up-tempo, the way he controls the ball, keeps his dribble. That creates a lot of opportunities for everybody else."[2]

In the first round of the playoffs, the Mavs faced the Minnesota Timberwolves. Minnesota was the No. 5 seed in the West, with a solid 50–32 record and All-Star forward Kevin Garnett and forward Wally Szczerbiak. Chauncey Billups, their point guard, had had a lot of success against the Mavs. Many people expected him to be a tough matchup for Nash in the first round. They were wrong.

Nash got the Mavs on track in Game 1 of the best-of-five series in Dallas. He drilled a 45-foot shot at the third-quarter buzzer to tie the game. The Mavs then rolled in the fourth quarter, winning 101–94. In Game 2, Nash had 10 assists and added 17 points as the Mavs won again, 122–110.

The Mavs took a 2–0 lead to Minnesota. They did not stay there long. The Mavs beat the Timberwolves 115–102 in Game 3 to complete the sweep.

STUMBLING BEFORE THE KINGS

The Mavs were confident heading into the second round. They had experience, having won a game against the San Antonio Spurs in a second-round series a year earlier. Their opponent this time would be the Sacramento Kings, the best team in the NBA during the regular season.

The Kings were a similar team to the Mavs. They employed a high-octane offense and did not bother to play much defense. They were led by forward Chris Webber and point guard Mike Bibby, another tough matchup for Nash.

The two teams braced for what was expected to be a competitive, exciting series. The Kings won Game 1 108–91, but the Mavs stole Game 2, 110–102, in Sacramento. Nash led the way. He scored 30 points while hitting 12 of 18 shots. He also tallied 8 assists in the upset.

Mark Bibby drives past Nash in a 2001 Kings win.

The series shifted for games 3 and 4 to Dallas, where the Mavs had been nearly unbeatable during the season. But it was the Kings who felt at home in Dallas. Sacramento won Game 3 despite 15 assists by Nash. The Kings also won Game 4, this time in overtime.

Nash was a big reason why the Mavs lost Game 4. He committed 9 turnovers. He was not much better when the teams returned to Sacramento for Game 5. Bibby held him to just 12 points, and the Kings took advantage, closing out the series with an easy 114–101 win.

Nash and the Mavs were disappointed when the best-of-seven series ended. Although the Kings had been favored, the Mavs expected to do better than a 4–1 series loss. Nash was especially upset. He averaged more than 4 turnovers per game during the series. Many experts pointed to Bibby's better play as a key reason why the Kings won easily.

"It's really sad and disappointing," Nash said. "We just had a few minutes in each game where we played uncharacteristically, and the season was gone like that."[3]

RENEWING THEIR DETERMINATION

The sting of losing to the Kings stayed with Nash through the off-season. When he and his teammates returned for the 2002–03 season, they were determined to use that disappointment as motivation.

That strategy worked. The Mavs won their first fourteen games of the season and built a big lead in the Midwest Division. They finished with 60 wins, setting a new franchise record. They earned the No. 3 seed in the West, finishing tied for first in the Midwest Division. They also led the NBA in scoring, had the league's best road record at 27–14, and won 36 games by at least 10 points.

Nash enjoyed a terrific season. He was again named an All-Star and averaged 17.7 points and 7.3 assists per game. During one stretch, he set a franchise record by making 49 straight free throws, and he shot better than 90 percent from the line for the season. He also posted 19 double-doubles, reaching double figures in both scoring and assists in a game.

MAVERICKS' MOST WINS IN A REGULAR SEASON IN 26-YEAR FRANCHISE HISTORY

60 (2002–03* and 2005–06)
58 (2004–05)
57 (2001–02)*
55 (1986–87)
53 (2000–01* and 1987–88)
* with Steve Nash on roster

Nash was named to the All-NBA third team. In December he was given the Lionel Conacher Award as the best Canadian male athlete in the world. He was the first basketball player to receive that honor.

"To be athlete of the year over all those great hockey players is really a big thrill for me," Nash said.[4]

Portland Trail Blazers forward Dale Davis (left) fouls Steve Nash as the Maverick guard tries to grab a loose ball.

The Mavs drew the Portland Trail Blazers in the first round of the 2003 NBA Playoffs. The Blazers had won 50 games during the regular season to earn the No. 6 seed. They were led by forward Rasheed Wallace and point guard Damon Stoudamire, the former Arizona guard who played against Nash in the 1993 NCAA Tournament.

At first Nash and the Mavs had no problems with Portland. They won the first game by 10 points. Game 2 was tight until Nash drilled a late three-pointer. His big shot broke a tie in the final minute. That, plus his 28 points, 8 assists, and 2 free throws with 14.5 seconds to play, helped the Mavs hold off the Blazers, 103–99.

DID YOU KNOW?
The Mavs again led the NBA in scoring (103 points per game) in 2002–03, improving their defense (95.2 points allowed) to 15th in the 29-team NBA.

The Mavs then won Game 3 by 12 points to take a 3–0 lead in the series. But thanks to an NBA rule change that season, the first round of playoffs was no longer a best-of-five series. The first round was now the same as the following rounds. Each was a best-of-seven series. That meant the Mavs still needed to win one more game to knock off the Blazers.

It took them a while. The Blazers won Game 4 at home in Portland and rallied to steal Game 5 in Dallas. Then the Blazers won Game 6 at home, tying the series at three games apiece.

The Mavs faced a must-win situation in Game 7. If they lost, not only would they lose the series and bow out of the playoffs in the first round, they would become the first team in NBA Playoff history to blow a 3–0 lead in a seven-game series.

But that pressure did not affect them. They played Game 7 loose and free at home, beating the Blazers

107–95. Nash scored 21 points and added 7 assists and 6 rebounds in the win.

ANOTHER CHANCE AGAINST THE KINGS

The Mavs moved on to a rematch against the Kings in the second round. This time they had two distinct advantages over Sacramento that they did not have in 2002. First, they had home-court advantage after winning more regular season games. Second, Webber would miss most of the series because of an injury.

The Mavs were a slight favorite, but it would not be easy. The Kings still had several solid players besides Webber, including Bibby, shooting guard Peja Stojakovich, center Vlade Divac, and guard Bobby Jackson.

The teams split games 1 and 2 in Dallas, with Webber succumbing to a knee injury in Game 2. He would miss the rest of the series. Nash scored 31 in Game 3 as the Mavs rallied to edge the Kings 141–137 in double overtime. The Kings then evened the series by winning Game 4.

NASH VS. KINGS' POINT GUARD MIKE BIBBY IN THE NBA PLAYOFFS, 2002, 2003, AND 2004

Overall averages per game:

Bibby: 18.4 points, 5.1 assists

Nash: 17.4 points, 8.9 assists

Bibby and the Kings won 2 of 3 series.

Steve Nash works the ball in the final moments of Game 2 in the Western Conference semifinal game against the Kings on May 6, 2002.

Nash led the way with 25 points and a career playoff high 7 rebounds as the Mavs rolled in Game 5 to retake the series lead. Nash made 15 of 16 free throws in the game, adding 4 assists and committing only one turnover as Dallas won 112–93. But the Kings won Game 6 to force a decisive Game 7.

Once again, Dallas got to play a deciding game at home. They used that to their advantage, ripping the Kings 112–99 before a boisterous crowd at the American Airlines Center. Nash set a new career playoff high with 13 assists and scored 18 as the Mavs advanced to the Western Conference Finals for the first time since 1988.

For Nash, Nowitzki, Finley, and coach Don Nelson, beating the Kings was the reward of several years of building. The Mavs were now one of only four teams still alive in the NBA Playoffs. That was a far cry from their 19–31 season in 1998–99. In only four years they had gone from a doormat to an elite team.

MAVERICKS VS. KINGS 2003 WESTERN CONFERENCE SEMIFINAL

Game 1: Kings 124, Mavs 113

Game 2 Mavs 132, Kings 110

Game 3: Mavs 141, Kings 137, double-overtime

Game 4: Kings 99, Mavs 83

Game 5: Mavs 112, Kings 93

Game 6: Kings 115, Mavs 109

Game 7: Mavs 112, Kings 99

"I was here in the dog days when twenty wins were considered a successful season," Finley said. "For us to come that far in such a short time is very gratifying for me."[5]

CHALLENGING THE SPURS

Next up for the Mavs was another old nemesis: the Spurs. San Antonio had eliminated the three-time defending champion Los Angeles Lakers in the second round, winning in six games. They had also edged the Mavs for the Midwest Division title on a tie-breaker and had defeated Dallas in the playoffs two years earlier.

The Mavs stole Game 1 in San Antonio, 113–110, rallying from an 18-point deficit. Nash scored 22. The Spurs then gained control of the series. They won the next three games, including two in Dallas, to take a 3–1 lead.

With Game 5 scheduled for San Antonio, the basketball world braced for a certain Spurs victory and talked about their expected return to the NBA Finals.

The Spurs' Tony Parker guards Steve Nash in a 2002 game.

Charles Barkley, an analyst on a popular TNT pre-game show, even said the Mavs were ready to "go fishing," meaning their season would soon be done, and they could go on vacation.

That appeared to be the case when the Mavs fell behind by 19 points early in Game 5 on the road. But these were a resilient bunch of Mavs. Nash scored 14 points and dished out 6 assists as Dallas rallied to beat the Spurs, 103–91.

"We gave them our not-go-fishing defense," Van Exel said. "And I don't fish anyway."[6]

The teams returned to Dallas for Game 6. The Mavs led for most of the game and still had a 13-point lead early in the fourth quarter. Then the Spurs caught fire, especially reserve guard Steve Kerr. Kerr hit 3 three-pointers in the quarter as the Spurs went on a 23–0 run and rallied to edge the Mavs 90–78.

Their season over, the Mavs were disappointed. But there was much to celebrate about the 2002–03 season. They had posted arguably the best season in the franchise's twenty-three-year history and advanced to a conference finals. They had a core of talented young players who proved they could succeed against the best in the league. They had battled the Spurs, who eventually won another NBA title, close to a standstill.

"I was hired here to turn the franchise around and we've done a pretty good job of doing that,"

Nelson said. "We're not world champions yet, or anything like that, but we're on our way and we still have work to do."[7]

Nash was disappointed, but he later realized just how far he and the Mavs had come.

"Truth is we had a tremendous year," Nash said. "We won a lot of games. Not many teams can say they won as many games as we did or played as long as we did. You have to fight yourself a little to not be too hard on yourself. As long as we stay motivated and continue to improve, we'll be fine."[8]

There was every reason to think that the Mavs would be fine. Yet the 2002–03 season would stand as Nash's finest achievement in his career as a Dallas Maverick—a career that would soon come to abrupt end.

CHAPTER EIGHT

Sharing His Wealth

Steve Nash is known around the world for his skills as a basketball player. He is one of the top point guards in the NBA.

Nash is also one of the finest people who play in the league. Ever since he became a professional basketball player in 1996, Nash has tried to use his popularity and wealth to help others.

THE STEVE NASH FOUNDATION

In 2001, Nash started the Steve Nash Foundation, which raises money to help underserved children improve their health, education, and lifestyle. His sister, Joann, and a high school friend help him run it.

Steve Nash high-fives a young basketball player during a break from the action at his charity basketball event in 2005.

The core program of Nash's foundation is his annual charity basketball game, the Steve Nash Foundation Charity Classic, which he holds every July. The 2005 game raised $300,000.

Nash, a few Suns teammates, and other NBA stars played a fast-paced game in front of a large crowd in Toronto that year. They made it a very

THE STEVE NASH FOUNDATION

Formed in 2001

Serves underprivileged kids

Signature event: Steve Nash Foundation Charity Classic held every July

Raised $300,000 in July 2005 game

entertaining event. Several thousand people watched as they played a lot of flashy offense but little defense. At one point, Nash displayed his soccer skills, dribbling the basketball with his feet to start a fast break.

Earlier on the day of that game, Nash donated $100,000 worth of shoes and other sports equipment to a community center in Toronto. The 2006 Nash Charity Classic was scheduled for July 22 in Vancouver, and Nash plans for future games to be held in Canada every July.

A GIVING HEART

Nash's charity work does not end there. He is glad to pitch in whenever possible. When New Jersey Nets forward Vince Carter had to miss his summer basketball camp once to attend U.S. Olympic team practices, he asked if Nash could take over. Nash did.

"He stole the show," Carter said. "That's beautiful. I told him I owe him one. I owe him one forever."[1]

After the Grizzlies moved from Vancouver to Memphis in 2002, the NBA franchise deserted a youth basketball league it had founded. Needing funding to continue, the league turned to Nash. He chipped in thousands of dollars to keep it afloat, and the league is now named after him. It is called the Steve Nash Youth Basketball League.

Nash has made helping youngsters a priority. He hopes that by funding the youth league, he will assist

Steve Nash takes part in a basketball camp in Vancouver, Canada.

Canadian cities in producing better players. Then more top Canadian high school players will have a better chance of landing basketball scholarships at American colleges than he did.

Nash volunteered for the Big Brothers/Big Sisters program when he lived in Dallas and spent time with kids who needed an older role model. In 1999, he donated $10,000 to a Dallas area YMCA to help improve its sports facilities for children.

There seems to be no limit to Nash's generosity. He recently donated several thousand dollars to the pediatric ward of a hospital in Asuncion, the capital city of Paraguay, where his wife grew up.

COUNTING HIS BLESSINGS

Meanwhile, Nash has tried to stay grounded and be the same person he was before he earned all the money and fame in the NBA.

"Life has changed to some extent," Nash said. "I feel pretty fortunate for everything that I've had and everything I've had an opportunity to work towards.

DID YOU KNOW?

Steve Nash suffers from a muscle condition known as spondylolisthesis. It makes his muscles tighten up and causes a lot of back pain. To combat the condition, Nash is constantly moving on the basketball court and often lies down, spreading out to keep his muscles from stiffening.

So although my lifestyle continues to change with, I guess, my success, it's something that I think I can make the most of and won't let bring me down."[2]

That means continuing to work hard and stay humble.

"Natural talent is only potential," he said. "You have to combine it with other things—confidence, hard work, even daring. . . . I try to come early every day to work. I put in a lot of time. When I get asked about the MVP, I feel uncomfortable saying something boastful. It would seem self-indulgent."[3]

His work ethic and modest personality are big reasons why Nash is so well-liked. He is honest and open with teammates, coaches, reporters, and fans. That has made him one of the game's most popular players and a role model.

Nash smiles after being named MVP in 2005.

SPEAKING HIS MIND

Nash's openness extends to his personal beliefs, as well. Some professional athletes hide their opinions, or do not have any, about important public issues.

That is not true for Nash. He often expresses his thoughts and feelings.

A famous example of that occurred during the 2003 NBA All-Star Game festivities in Atlanta. The All-Star Weekend took place in mid-February, while the United States government was considering launching a war on Iraq. Few pro athletes spoke up about this touchy subject.

Nash was not afraid to share his opinion. He wore a controversial T-shirt during a media conference before the game. The shirt read: "No War—Shoot for Peace."

The shirt showed Nash's belief that the United States should not go to war with Iraq. Nash wore it even though he knew he would probably be criticized by many people. He wore it because he felt it was important for him to use his celebrity status to start a public discussion.

". . . it's important for people to educate themselves on what is happening so that they can make informed decisions."

–Steve Nash

When reporters asked him about it, he explained his anti-war feelings in detail. He never avoided their questions.

"I didn't take a stand on the war to tell people how to think, or to tell them what to believe in, or to draw attention to myself," Nash said. "I just feel that in the present international state of affairs, it's important for people to educate themselves on what is happening so that they can make informed decisions."[4]

Some people ripped Nash for expressing his opinions. One prominent sports columnist wrote:

"Steve Nash of the Dallas Mavericks should just shut up and play. . . . You often see this in the heavily hero-worshipped arenas of acting and athletics. A star deludes himself or herself into believing that his or her ability to entertain millions qualifies him or her to solve the world's problems and lead the country."[5]

David Robinson, the Spurs' center and a graduate of the U.S. Naval Academy, criticized Nash and a Mavs teammate who was publicly anti-war a few weeks later. Robinson's comments came after the United States had declared war on Iraq in March of 2003.

"If [the war is] an embarrassment to them, maybe they should be in a different country," Robinson said. "This is America, and we're supposed to be proud of the guys we elected and put into office."[6]

Yet many other people defended Nash. They included teammates Nick Van Exel and Tariq Abdul-Wahad and prominent sports columnist Gwen Knapp of the *San Francisco Chronicle*.

DID YOU KNOW?
The United States declared war on Iraq on March 19, 2003, late in the NBA's regular season.

"Now on the court, he continues to be a spectacular leader for Dallas," Knapp wrote, "proving that some athletes can have a world view without taking their eyes off the ball."[7]

Two years later, Nash was still being praised for speaking his mind.

"His refusal to shy away from the pulpit that comes with being a public figure and his embrace of an unpopular stance at a time when this country was in virtual lockstep with the Bush administration showed guts," said one writer. "Nash plays the game of life right."[8]

Whether people agreed with Nash's beliefs or not, it is clear that he has gained respect for not being afraid to voice them.

It was no surprise that people came to Nash's defense. Besides being popular among fans, he is also very well-liked among his teammates, coaches, and other NBA players. Nash's friendship with Nowitzki and Finley has been well-documented, but he has also quickly made friends with several of his Suns teammates. How else could he have become a team leader so quickly in his return to Phoenix?

"Steve's a great guy," teammate Amare Stoudemire said.[9]

"I love being part of a team, any team," Nash said. "Not just playing, but the camaraderie, the whole thing."[10]

MORE THAN JUST A SPORTS STAR

Nash is also a well-rounded person. He reads often, including books by European philosophers, and he speaks Spanish at home with his wife and at work with teammate Leandro Barbosa. He also travels as much as he can in the off-season. He has been to places in Europe, Central America, South America, the Caribbean, and several other locations.

"Whenever I travel, I feel almost calm. I love people. I love the world," Nash said.[11]

Nash also spends time in the off-season playing pickup games of basketball and soccer. He enjoys hanging out at his suburban Phoenix home with his wife and two young daughters. During one off-season, he played pickup soccer games in New York, then treated everyone—his teammates and competitors—to meals afterward.

SOME PLACES STEVE NASH HAS BEEN:

Paraguay, Australia, England, Puerto Rico, The Dominican Republic, Argentina, Brazil, and Nicaragua

That is yet another example of Nash's generosity. In fact, after he retires he

OTHER STEVE NASH FAVORITES

Hockey team: The old Edmonton Oilers teams of the 1980s, featuring his favorite player, center Wayne Gretzky

Bands: Radiohead, the Rolling Stones, and David Bowie

wants to start a career as a philanthropist. That means he wants to aid and assist people for a living.

Nash's thoughtfulness and zest for life have rubbed off on people. In May 2006, he received an honor perhaps more important than his NBA MVP awards. *Time Magazine* named him one of the 100 most influential people in the world, placing him on a list that included such prominent people as Senator John McCain and former president Bill Clinton.

Nash was one of only three professional athletes on the list. *Time* said he is one of the "global icons . . . who are using their influence to do the right thing."[12] Charles Barkley, a TNT analyst and a former Suns forward, wrote a short essay about why Nash is one of the 100 people who most shapes the world.

"I'm glad the world has got a chance to learn from a guy like Steve Nash," Barkley wrote. "Who knows? Maybe he'll inspire a whole new generation of kids to pass out of double teams the way he does. Like Nash, maybe they'll be selfless off the court, too. That would be even better."[13]

CHAPTER NINE

Back With the Suns

After their breakout 2002–03 season, the Mavs hoped to contend again for an NBA championship in 2003–04. They returned their "Big Three" of Nash, Nowitzki, and Finley, but the team's management decided to make changes in the rest of the roster.

The Mavs went for broke. They dealt Van Exel and others for high-scoring forwards Antoine Walker and Antawn Jamison. Their strategy was to try to outscore teams. The moves gave the Mavs the league's best offense, but they hurt the team chemistry and did not help the defense. As a result, it was an up-and-down season.

STEVE NASH ★ LEADER ON AND OFF THE COURT

A DISAPPOINTING SEASON

The Mavs again won more than 50 games and contended for the Midwest Division title. But they finished third in the division, behind the Spurs and the Timberwolves, and placed fifth in the Western Conference. That was their lowest finish in the West in three years.

MAVS CHANGES FOR 2003–04 SEASON (FROM 2002–03 ROSTER)

In: Antoine Walker, Antawn Jamison, Travis Best, Marquis Daniels, Tony Delk, Danny Fortson, Josh Howard, Jon Stefansson, Scott Williams

Out: Raef LaFrentz, Nick Van Exel, Raja Bell, Evan Eschmeyer, Adrian Griffin, Avery Johnson, Popeye Jones, Antoine Rigaudeau, Walt Williams

Nash set new career highs in assists in a game, collecting 19 in an April win against the Kings, and assists per game in a season with 8.8. He recorded his first career triple-double, notching double figures in points, assists, and rebounds. In a November win against Portland, he scored 14 points to go with 12 assists and 10 rebounds. Yet for the season, Nash averaged only 14.5 points, his lowest output in four years.

After he played in all 82 games in both the 2001–02 and 2002–03 seasons, Nash missed four games due to injury in 2003–04. A shoulder injury

Steve Nash drives for a shot against Sacramento Kings center Vlade Divac in Game 5 of the Western Conference semifinals May 13, 2003.

forced him to sit out a November 6 game in Toronto, ending his consecutive-games streak at 195.

Things got worse in the playoffs. The Mavs again faced the Kings, this time in the first round. The result was similar to 2002. The Kings won the first two games in Sacramento. The teams split games 3 and 4 in Dallas, but the Kings closed out the series by winning Game 5 back in Sacramento.

> **DID YOU KNOW?**
> The Mavs again led the NBA in scoring with 105.2 points per game in 2003–04, but they slipped to 28th in scoring defense with 100.8 points allowed. They committed the fewest turnovers in the league.

The most disappointing thing was not that the Mavs lost the series. It was that they had a great chance to win three of the four games that they lost. In each one, they failed to make a key play late in the game. That failure mirrored their season.

"It was a struggle all season," Nelson said. "I never got this team where I wanted them."[1]

BACK TO THE SUNS

The Mavs' 2003–04 experiment failed. Now they had a lot of problems to resolve. One of them was what to do with Nash, their captain, an All-Star, and the face of the franchise.

Nash opted out of his contract before the season, making him a free agent after the Mavs lost to the Kings. He was thirty years old, with eight seasons of NBA experience, a history of nagging back injuries, and one glaring negative statistic: Nash played an average of about 34 minutes per game in each of his last four seasons in Dallas. Many top point guards in the NBA, by comparison, play more than 40 minutes per game.

Nelson often sat Nash for long stretches of games because he wanted to keep Nash fresh for the fourth quarter. The small Nash would not be able to play as well, Nelson thought, if his body had to take the pounding that an NBA point guard typically takes during 40 minutes or more of play. That was especially true because of Nash's style of play. He would often crash into much bigger, taller players in an effort to help the Mavs score.

Mavs owner Mark Cuban noted Nash's reduced workload, injury history, a reputation of tiring during the playoffs, and the fact that Kings guard Bibby had outplayed him in two of three recent playoff series. Cuban would not give Nash a maximum contract, he said, because of those reasons and a fear that Nash's play would diminish as he aged into his thirties.

Cuban was prepared to offer Nash several million dollars per season, for four or five years. It would be a generous offer, but Nash got a better one elsewhere.

In July 2004, Nash's agent arranged a meeting with the Phoenix Suns. The Suns were Nash's old team and had drafted him eight years earlier. They had a different coach and all new

Nash drives through an accidental kick by a defender.

players by now, but the Suns' management knew how valuable Nash was.

At the meeting in Phoenix, the Suns offered Nash $55 million to play for five years. Nash gave the Mavs an opportunity to match the offer. They refused, so Nash signed a new contract to play for the Suns.

Nash was excited to return to Phoenix. He already knew the city a bit, and his parents and a few old friends from Canada owned homes in the area. The Suns, meanwhile, planned to employ a fast-paced offense similar to Dallas' and wanted Nash to be the leader of their young team.

"When you think about it, it is really weird," Nash said. "I was just part of a bunch of guys in Dallas who came in together and helped change things. Now, it's a different role for me, all of a sudden. I can handle it, I understand it, but it is definitely different. I'm the old man here."[2]

A DIFFICULT FAREWELL

Before he moved back to Phoenix, though, Nash had to say good-bye to friends in Dallas. That was difficult. He had grown close to Nowitzki and Finley. They had a lot of success together after enduring a tough rebuilding process.

"The only thing that hurt me is having to leave my buddies—leaving the team that we helped build together," Nash said. "I wanted to finish my career [in Dallas]. I wanted to play with two of my best friends."[3]

In Dallas, Nash worked hard to be a better player and to help the Mavs improve.

THE BIG THREE'S RECORDS
1998–99: 19–31
1999–2000: 40–42
2000–01: 53–29, advanced to second round of playoffs
2001–02: 57–25, advanced to second round of playoffs
2002–03: 60–22, advanced to Western Conference Finals
2003–04: 52–30, lost in first round of playoffs

"To do that with guys that you are close with—talented guys—that doesn't happen very often in this league," Nash said. "We were very fortunate for that, and too bad it couldn't keep going."[4]

The Mavs were appreciative of what Nash, Nowitzki, and Finley did together.

"They were one of the more special triads to ever lace them up in the league," Mavs president Don

THE BIG THREE'S LEGACY
Nowitzki, Nash, and Finley in Dallas, 1998–2004:
Mavs record: 281–179 (.611 wining percentage)
Took Mavs to conference finals for first time in 15 years (2003)
Mavs led NBA in scoring three times
Mavs posted a 19–24 record in the playoffs

Nelson said. "They enjoyed playing with each other and that certainly had a whole lot to do with elevating the Mavericks as a franchise over the years that they were together. So I'm sure that Steve will be missed.

"They got through those tough years together, and, as a result, after weathering the hard years, they really helped this franchise turn the corner and really kind of defined where it is today."[6]

THE BIG THREE INDIVIDUAL NUMBERS, PER-GAME AVERAGES (1998–2004)

Michael Finley: 19.3 points, 5.2 rebounds, 3.8 assists

Dirk Nowitzki: 20.4 points, 8.3 rebounds

Steve Nash: 12.7 points, 6 assists

SILENCING THE CRITICS

When Nash signed the new deal with the Suns, a lot of basketball experts criticized the team for overpaying him. Nash, they said, was too old and brittle. He would never lead a team to an NBA title.

Nash carried the weight of trying to revive the Suns. The franchise had never won an NBA title and had not advanced as far as the Western Conference Finals since 1993. Besides that heavy burden, Nash also had to deal with personal changes in 2004. He was moving again. His girlfriend gave birth to twin daughters, and he got married soon after he became a father. As usual, the relaxed Nash took the changes and pressure in stride.

"Moving cities, changing teams, buying a new house and having children, it's nice to do it all at once," Nash said. "In some ways, you can adjust to it right away and get used to it instead of having changes every year and never really feeling like your life is settled."[7]

Nash, it turned out, was just the player Phoenix needed to transform into an NBA title contender. The Suns had won only 29 games in 2003–04. But they had a young coach, Mike D'Antoni, who, like Don Nelson, was not afraid to let Nash run the offense as he pleased. They also had rising stars in forward Shawn Marion and center Amare Stoudemire.

Nash immediately clicked with his new teammates. The Suns got off to a torrid start in 2004–05, winning 31 of their first 35 games. Nash was named the NBA Player of the Month for November, the season's opening month. On November 16, he led the Suns to a 107–101 win against his old teammates in Dallas and scored 17 points while adding 18 assists.

The Suns opened up a huge lead in the Pacific Division and won it easily. For the season, they won 62 games, tying a franchise record for most wins in a season. They posted the best record of any NBA team

Nash had ever played on and earned the No. 1 seed in the Western Conference.

Nash had a terrific season. He was named an All-Star and won the skills challenge during All-Star Weekend. He averaged 15.5 points and a career high 11.5 assists per game. That was nearly a full three assists per game more than his previous career high, which he had set the year before in Dallas. He also set a new single-game career high by pulling down 13 rebounds in a March win against the Philadelphia 76ers.

During the playoffs, the NBA named Nash its Most Valuable Player for the regular season. That was quite an honor, especially for a player who had been booed twice early in his career and written off often.

"He is this year's MVP," Milwaukee Bucks guard Michael Redd said. "He's just phenomenal—the premier point guard in the league, no question."[8]

THE PHOENIX SUNS BEFORE STEVE NASH:

2001–02: 36–46, no playoffs

2002–03: 44–38, lost in first round of NBA Playoffs

2003–04: 29–53, no playoffs

The Suns with Nash:

2004–05: 62–20, advanced to conference finals

DID YOU KNOW?

The Suns led the NBA in scoring in 2004–05 with 112 points per game, marking the fourth straight year that a team with Steve Nash at point guard was the league's top scorer. The Suns also led the NBA in field goal percentage with an average of .493.

Nash holds his 2005
MVP trophy.

"They have to be crazy to let that boy go," Suns forward Quentin Richardson said of the Mavs. "Thank you, Dallas! I'm glad to be on his team."[9]

MEETING HIS OLD TEAM IN THE PLAYOFFS

In the playoffs, the Suns swept the Memphis Grizzlies in four games in the first round. Nash averaged 11.3 assists and 15 points in the series as the Suns advanced, setting up a second-round matchup with the Mavs.

Dallas was a vastly different team than the unit that Nash had led for several seasons. Nowitzki and Finley were still there, but players such as Van Exel, Walker, and Jamison were gone.

In their place were veteran players such as Jerry Stackhouse and Keith Van Horn, as well as new young players. The Mavs acquired two point guards to replace Nash: Jason Terry, a top scorer whom Dallas got in a trade with the Atlanta Hawks, and Devin Harris, a rookie they acquired in a trade with the Washington Wizards. The Mavs were now coached by Avery Johnson, Nash's former teammate. Don Nelson had retired during the regular season.

The Mavs were eager to show Nash that they did not miss him. They believed Harris and

DID YOU KNOW?

When the Mavs faced the Suns in the 2005 NBA Playoffs, only five of fourteen Mavs players had been Steve Nash's teammates the year before in Dallas.

Steve Nash gets around Dallas Mavericks forward Dirk Nowitzki in the fourth quarter of their game in Dallas November 16, 2004.

Terry could take the Mavs further in the playoffs than Nash ever did. Nash wanted to prove to the Mavs that he was not a playoff choker. He wanted to show a championship team could be built around him even though he was in his thirties.

The Suns won two of the first three games of the series, taking games 1 and 3 easily and narrowly losing in Game 2. During the first three games, Nash continued to play as he had during the regular season, getting his teammates the ball instead of looking for his own shot.

THE 2004–05 SEASON, NASH'S FIRST BACK IN PHOENIX

Mavericks 58–24, lost to Suns in second round of NBA Playoffs

Suns 62–20, beat Mavericks in second round, lost to Spurs in Western Conference Finals

Then, it was as if he had another meeting with Nelson, like the one in 2000 that inspired him to become more of an offensive force. Beginning in Game 4, Nash shot the ball a lot more—and made many more shots. His sudden change in play shaped the outcome of the series.

Dallas won Game 4, 119–109. But Nash scored 48 points. In 44 minutes, he made 20 of 28 field goals and all 4 free throws he attempted. Nash was even more effective in Game 5. He recorded the first triple-double of his playoff career, scoring 34 points and handing out 12 assists to go with 13 rebounds. The Suns won 114–108 in Phoenix.

THE 2005 WESTERN CONFERENCE SEMIFINALS, DALLAS VS. PHOENIX

Game 1: Suns 127, Mavs 102
Game 2: Mavs 108, Suns 106
Game 3: Suns 119, Mavs 102
Game 4: Mavs 119, Suns 109
Game 5: Suns 114, Mavs 108
Game 6: Suns 130, Mavs 126, overtime

The Suns sought to close out the series in Dallas in Game 6. They trailed by sixteen points late in the third quarter but drew within three in the final seconds. Nash then drilled a three-pointer to force overtime. The Suns outscored the Mavs 19–15 in the extra session to win, 130–126. Playing almost the entire game, Nash scored 39 points on 14-of-24 shooting and had 12 assists.

For the series, he averaged 12 assists and more than 30 points per game. He was universally praised.

NASH'S STATS IN SEMIFINAL SERIES VS. DALLAS

Game 1: 11 points, 13 assists, 6 rebounds

Game 2: 23 points, 13 assists, 3 rebounds

Game 3: 27 points, 17 assists, 3 rebounds

Game 4: 48 points, 5 assists, 5 rebounds

Game 5: 34 points, 12 assists, 13 rebounds

Game 6: 39 points, 12 assists, 9 rebounds

"Wasn't Nash the guy who, according to local legend, wore out in the postseason?" wrote a Dallas sports columnist. "Fifty minutes. That was Nash's court time in Game 6, and he was as strong at the end as at the start."[9]

"He made some unbelievable plays," Nowitzki said of Nash. "Every game they won he was phenomenal. I've never seen him play better than this. He really wanted to show all of Dallas what we missed."[10]

It was sweet vindication for Nash. He led the Suns back to the conference finals in only his first season in Phoenix. He did it at the expense of his former team in front of his former fans, with Cuban, the owner who did not want him, watching from a courtside seat. Fitting his personality, though, Nash did not feel too jubilant after the series.

NASH'S STATS IN THE 2005 NBA PLAYOFFS

Nash started and played in 15 games. He averaged 23.9 points, 11.3 assists, and 4.8 rebounds per game.

Nash is closely guarded by Dirk Nowitzki.

"It was difficult to have to see them go home," Nash said of his old teammates.[11]

THE SEASON ENDS

In the conference finals, the Suns met an opponent familiar to Nash: the Spurs. San Antonio won the series in five games on their way to winning another NBA championship. Nash was disappointed to see the season end so suddenly, but he was proud of his first season back in Phoenix.

"This has been an incredible year for me and for our team," Nash said.[12]

Nash could not wait to see if he could take the Suns further in 2005–06, and if he could defend his MVP award. He had no idea how difficult meeting those goals would be.

Still Competing for an NBA Title

After taking a huge leap in the 2004–05 season, the Suns hoped to take the next step in 2005–06 and reach the NBA Finals.

With Nash, the reigning NBA MVP, and standouts Shawn Marion and Amare Stoudemire returning, they were a consensus pick to repeat as Pacific Division champions and push the Spurs for the Western Conference title. The Suns made a few changes in the off-season to improve their defense. They brought in veteran forwards Kurt Thomas and Brian Grant. They later added forward Tim Thomas.

Yet the Suns would never get the chance to face the Spurs, or any team, at full strength in 2005–06.

PLAYING SHORT-HANDED

The Suns' chances of winning an NBA title suffered a major blow before the season started when Stoudemire suffered a knee injury. He was lost for several months and returned after the All-Star break. But he played in just three games before the injury sidelined him for the rest of the season.

The Suns also lost Grant and Kurt Thomas for long stretches of the season to injury. The Suns were often forced to play with only a seven-man rotation. That meant D'Antoni would have to rely more on his starters, including Nash, who played more minutes during this season than any in his career. Nash averaged 35.5 minutes per game.

Many believed that Nash, who turned thirty-two during the season, could not hold up over so many minutes. With so many injuries and changes, some experts expected the Suns to relinquish the Pacific Division to the Los Angeles Clippers, Los Angeles Lakers, or Sacramento Kings.

Instead, the Suns again flourished. Young players, such as forward Boris Diaw and guard Leandro Barbosa, emerged. Nash and Marion continued to play at an elite level. The Suns won 54 games and captured a second straight division title. They earned the No. 2 seed in the Western Conference.

DID YOU KNOW?
The Suns were first in the NBA in scoring (108.4) in 2005–06 and again led the league in field goal percentage (.479). Only the Mavs, Nash's old team, scored more points (112.1).

Nash had another outstanding season. He compensated a bit for the loss of Stoudemire and averaged a career high 18.8 points and 10.5 assists. He was named an All-Star starter for the first time in his career. Whenever the Suns struggled, Nash kept them afloat.

Experts pointed to Nash as the main reason why the Suns did not slip despite losing Stoudemire. As a result, Nash was again named the NBA's MVP for the regular season. But he was tiring as the playoffs began.

BACK IN THE PLAYOFFS

In the first round, the Suns faced the Lakers, the No. 7 seed in the West. The Lakers were a far cry from the dominant team that won three straight NBA championships from 2000 to 2002. They still had All-NBA guard Kobe Bryant and talented players such as forward Lamar Odom, though.

After the Suns won Game 1, the Lakers seized the next two games. Phoenix led Game 4 late in the fourth quarter, but, in the final seconds, Nash was stripped of the ball, and Bryant made a game-tying layup to force overtime.

In overtime Nash made a go-ahead three-pointer with 50 seconds to play. But again he was victimized. With the Suns up by one point in the final seconds, two Lakers surrounded him and battled him for the ball. Officials called a jump ball. Nash lost the jump, and the Lakers got the ball to Bryant. He dribbled past half court to a spot about 17 feet from the basket. Bryant buried a buzzer-beating jumper to give the Lakers a 99–98 win.

Down 3–1, the Suns had to win three straight games to take the series. Few teams in NBA playoff history had ever done that. However, the Suns did not despair. Nash scored 22 points as his team won Game 5 at home 114–97.

In Game 6, Nash was magnificent. He scored 32 points and handed out 13 assists as the Suns and Lakers battled back and forth. The Lakers led by three points in the waning seconds, but Tim Thomas nailed a three-pointer to tie the game and send it into overtime. In the extra session, Thomas and Diaw hit big shots as the Suns outlasted the Lakers 126–118.

Game 7 was no contest. The Suns took a big early lead and rolled to a 121–90 win. Nash scored 13 points and had 9 assists. He rested for much of the fourth quarter as the Suns advanced to the second round again.

"I have to say, I'm really proud of our team," Nash said.[1]

The Suns drew L.A.'s other team, the Clippers, in the second round. The Clippers were led by All-Star forward Elton Brand and veteran guard Sam Cassell, who had played with Nash briefly in Phoenix during the 1996–97 season. The Clippers had crushed the Denver Nuggets in the first round and, playing at full strength, presented a formidable opponent.

The series would prove to be one of the most entertaining NBA Playoff series in years. The teams traded wins for the first four games.

In Game 5, the host Suns blew a late lead, allowing the Clippers to force overtime. The Suns fell behind in the extra session. With just seconds to play, they trailed by three points. Then, guard Raja Bell took an inbounds pass and drilled a three-pointer from the corner, tying the game and forcing a second overtime. The Suns controlled the second overtime period, edging the Clippers 125–118. Nash played 50 of 58 minutes in the game, dishing out 13 assists to go with 17 points.

After losing Game 6 in L.A., the Suns returned home for Game 7. They benefited from a few extra days of rest due to an NBA scheduling quirk. Nash, who had admitted to being tired in Game 6, played at the top of his game. He hit 11 of 16 shots to score 29 points. He added 11 assists as the Suns beat the Clippers, 127–107, to win the series.

"We are a resilient team," Nash said. "We have been through a lot this year with injuries and lack of size, whatever you want to talk about. We have overcome a lot and we have turned out to be a really good team."[2]

FACING THE MAVS AGAIN

The Suns were back in the Western Conference Finals for the second straight season. This marked the first time in sixteen years the franchise had accomplished that feat. Their reward was another tilt with the Mavs.

The 2005–06 Mavs were arguably the best team in franchise history. They matched the franchise's record for most victories in a regular season with 60, set by Nash's 2002–03 Mavs. They boasted a balanced ten-man rotation and had home-court advantage for the series against Phoenix.

Nash relished the opportunity to advance to his first NBA Finals at the expense of his former team. Nash and Nowitzki, the old friends, were now battling each other in order to get the one thing that neither of them had: an NBA title.

The Mavs appeared to be the better team in Game 1. They led for most of the second half and took a nine-point lead late in the fourth quarter. Then Nash rallied the Suns. First he drove by Nowitzki and made a difficult layup. Then, he drained a pair of three-pointers and two free throws. Nash scored nine points in the final four minutes. Overall, he scored 27 points and had 16 assists as the Suns rallied for a 121–118 victory.

Nash looks to pass in a May 18, 2005, game.

**THE 2006 WESTERN
CONFERENCE FINALS**

Game 1: Suns 121, Mavs 118

Game 2: Mavs 105, Suns 98

Game 3: Mavs 95, Suns 88

Game 4: Suns 106, Mavs 86

Game 5: Mavs 117, Suns 101

Game 6: Mavs 102, Suns 93

The Mavs regrouped and won the next two games. In Game 4, Nash scored 21 and added 7 assists as the Suns easily won the contest and evened the series. The series had boiled down to a best-of-three.

It would be Nowitzki's turn to compete for the title first. The Mavs trailed for most of Game 5. But Nowitzki, who scored 50 points, keyed a fourth-quarter explosion, and Dallas rallied to win. Game 6 was almost a carbon copy of Game 5. The Suns led for most of the game, but Dallas rallied late and stole the game—and the series.

Immediately after the game, Nash embraced Nowitzki near midcourt. If somebody had to make it to the NBA Finals besides the Suns, Nash thought, at least it was Dirk.

**STEVE NASH'S STATS IN 2006
WESTERN CONFERENCE FINALS**

Game 1: 27 points, 16 assists

Game 2: 16 points, 11 assists

Game 3: 21 points, 7 assists

Game 4: 21 points, 7 assists

Game 5: 20 points, 11 assists

Game 6: 19 points, 9 assists

"They had an incredible year," Dallas coach Avery Johnson said of the Suns. "Nash is such a special player. I had to change my pick-and-roll coverage every time down the court. It was a special run, especially without Stoudemire."[3]

REMAINING HOPEFUL

For the second straight year, the Suns fell two steps short of an NBA championship, extending an NBA title drought for the franchise and Nash. Having participated in 86 playoff games, Nash holds the record as the only active NBA player to compete in so many playoff games without winning an NBA title. He has played ten seasons in the NBA without even making it to the NBA Finals.

Still, the Suns had an impressive corps of young players coming back and Nash as their leader. Nash remained as optimistic as ever about his chances for winning a championship.

"We're pretty close," Nash said. "We can all improve individually and collectively. So [losing to Dallas is] not the end of the world.[4]

"I think we proved we can win a championship playing this way. We were right there."[5]

CAREER STATISTICS

YEAR	TEAM	G	GS	MIN	FGM–A	3PM–A	FTM–A
96–97	Phoenix	65	2	684	74–175	23–55	42–51
97–98	Phoenix	76	9	1,664	268–584	81–195	74–86
98–99	Dallas	40	40	1,269	114–314	49–131	38–46
99–00	Dallas	56	27	1,532	173–363	60–149	75–85
00–01	Dallas	70	70	2,387	386–792	89–219	231–258
01–02	Dallas	82	82	2,837	525–1,088	156–343	260–293
02–03	Dallas	82	82	2,711	518–1,114	111–269	308–339
03–04	Dallas	78	78	2,612	397–845	104–257	230–251
04–05	Phoenix	75	75	2,573	430–857	94–218	211–238
05–06	Phoenix	79	79	2,796	541–1,056	150–342	257–279
Career		703	544	21,065	3,426–7,188	917–2,178	1,726–1,926
Playoff		86	79	3,093	534–1,140	134–326	272–302
All-Star		4	1	85	6–16	2–7	0–1

KEY:
G=Games Played
GS=Games Started
MIN=Minutes Played
FGM–A=Field Goals Made–Attempted
3PM–A=Three-Pointers Made–Attempted
FTM–A=Free Throws Made–Attempted
AST=Assists
STL=Steals
BLK=Blocks
TO=Turnovers
PF=Personal Fouls
PTS=Points

AST	STL	BLK	TO	PF	PTS
138	20	0	63	92	213
262	63	4	98	145	691
219	37	2	83	98	315
272	37	3	102	122	481
509	72	5	205	158	1,092
634	53	4	229	164	1,466
598	85	6	192	134	1,455
687	67	8	209	139	1,128
861	74	6	245	136	1,165
826	61	12	276	120	1,489
5,006	569	50	1,702	1,308	9,495
706	56	11	260	186	1,474
24	3	0	9	4	14

CAREER ACHIEVEMENTS

1992   Led St. Michael's to British Columbia high school provincial championship

1993   Named West Coast Conference (WCC) Tournament MVP

1993   Sank six late free throws to help Santa Clara shock Arizona in NCAA Tournament

1995   Named WCC Player of the Year

1996   Again named WCC Player of the Year

1996   Selected in first round of NBA Draft

1997–98   Led Phoenix Suns in three-point shooting percentage with an average of .415

2000	Led Team Canada to first-place finish in Group B at Summer Olympics
2002	Selected to first NBA All-Star Game
2003	Led Mavericks to first conference finals in fifteen years
2004–05	Led NBA in assists per game with an average of 11.5
2004–05	Named to All-NBA first team; voted NBA MVP
2005–06	Selected to start All-Star Game for first time; named to All-NBA first-team; voted NBA MVP again; led NBA in free-throw shooting (.921); led NBA in assists per game (10.5)

CHAPTER NOTES

CHAPTER 1. KEEPING HIS COOL

1. Associated Press report, "Nash named MVP again," *Los Angeles Times*, May 8, 2006.
2. Ibid.
3. Jack McCallum, "Point Guard From Another Planet," *Sports Illustrated*, January 30, 2006.
4. Ray Buck, "The Mavs' ramblin' man," *Fort Worth Star-Telegram*, April 21, 2003.
5. Mike McAllister, "Nash's high-energy style forces Mavs to fasten their seat belts," *Dallas Morning News*, February 9, 2003.
6. Steve Buffery, "MVP," *Toronto Sun*, January 30, 2005.
7. Juliet Macur, "AIR BUDS," *Dallas Morning News*, January 30, 2001.

CHAPTER 2. A GIFTED ATHLETE

1. Staff reports, "Suns' Nash still gets kick out of soccer," *USA TODAY*, November 5, 1997.
2. Richard Hoffer, "The Tao of Steve," *Sports Illustrated*, December 17, 2001.
3. Sean Gregory, with reporting by Wendy Long, "A Dash of Nash," *Time International*, May 16, 2005.
4. Ibid.
5. Ibid.
6. Jerry Crowe, "This Nash is a scrambler," *Los Angeles Times*, February 28, 1995.
7. Jack McCallum, "Point Guard From Another Planet," *Sports Illustrated*, January 30, 2006.
8. Tim Crothers, "Little Magic," *Sports Illustrated*, December 11, 1995.

CHAPTER 3. BECOMING A LEADER

1. J. A. Adande, "15th-Seeded Santa Clara Plants Arizona," *Los Angeles Times*, March 19, 1993.
2. Ivan Maisel, "Canadian Nash: American Flash," *Newsday*, March 15, 1996.
3. Tim Crothers, "Little Magic," *Sports Illustrated*, December 11, 1995.
4. Craig Daniels, "Nash Thriving in the Sun," *Toronto Sun*, February 4, 1998.
5. Tim Crothers, "Little Magic," *Sports Illustrated*, December 11, 1995.

CHAPTER 4. COMPETING FOR PLAYING TIME

1. Sam Farmer, "Nash, Suns Smiling," *San Jose Mercury News*, June 27, 1996.
2. Bud Geracie, "Hard-working Nash becomes Suns' rising star," *San Jose Mercury News*, January 22, 1998.
3. Michael Martinez, "Nash Rising With Suns," *San Jose Mercury News*, October 30, 1997.
4. Doug Smith, "Nash courts success," *Toronto Star*, February 1, 1998.
5. Michael Martinez, "Nash Rising With Suns," *San Jose Mercury News*, October 30, 1997.
6. "Pass happy," *Maclean's*, February 1999.
7. Ibid.

CHAPTER 5. STRUGGLING AS A MAVERICK

1. Frank Luksa, "Mavericks make sure all get good look at Nash," *Dallas Morning News*, June 30, 1998.
2. Marc Stein, "Nash gets 6-year, $33 million deal," *Dallas Morning News*, January 26, 1999.
3. Dwain Price, "Season to forget," *Fort Worth Star-Telegram*, October 7, 1999.
4. Ibid.
5. Ibid.
6. Marc Stein, "Nash tries to dish off home crowd's boos," *Dallas Morning News*, March 26, 1999.
7. Juliet Macur, "AIR BUDS," *Dallas Morning News*, January 30, 2001.
8. Ibid.
9. Marc Stein, "Mavericks happy to stay put in draft," *Dallas Morning News*, June 27, 1999.
10. Tim Cowlishaw, "Nash finally gives Nelson chance to make his point," *Dallas Morning News*, November 30, 2000.
11. Edie Sefko, "Nash edges O'Neal for MVP," *Dallas Morning News*, May 9, 2005.

CHAPTER 6. AN OLYMPIC TURNAROUND

1. Art Garcia, "Nash's World," *Fort Worth Star-Telegram*, August 27, 2003.
2. Marc Stein, "Nash is Canada's difference in 83–75 upset of Yugoslavia," *Dallas Morning News*, September 26, 2000.
3. Ed Willes, "Nash's flash nets Canada win over Russia," *Edmonton Journal*, September 30, 2000.
4. Juliet Macur, "AIR BUDS," *Dallas Morning News*, January 30, 2001.

5. Tim Cowlishaw, "Nash finally gives Nelson chance to make his point," *Dallas Morning News*, November 30, 2000.

6. Juliet Macur, "AIR BUDS," *Dallas Morning News*, January 30, 2001.

7. Brad Townsend, "Nash's winning shot shows something to Stockton, Jazz," *Dallas Morning News*, April 29, 2001.

8. Ibid.

9. Marc Stein, "Nash's gutsy fourth quarter helps lift Mavs," *Dallas Morning News*, May 4, 2001.

10. Dwain Price, "RALLY CAPPED," *Fort Worth Star-Telegram*, May 4, 2001.

11. Tim Cowlishaw, "Nash finally gives Nelson chance to make his point," *Dallas Morning News*, November 30, 2000.

CHAPTER 7. A TEAM PROVING ITSELF

1. Kevin Lyons, "Pivotal Point," *Fort Worth Star-Telegram*, April 6, 2002.

2. Ibid.

3. Brad Townsend, "One day later, Mavericks looking one season ahead," *Dallas Morning News*, May 15, 2002.

4. Neil Davidson, "NBA's Nash is top athlete," *Montreal Gazette*, December 27, 2002.

5. Dwain Price, "Earning their Spurs," *Fort Worth Star-Telegram*, May 18, 2003.

6. Randy Galloway, "Mavs' guts bigger, better than Barkley's," *Fort Worth Star-Telegram*, May 28, 2003.

7. Dwain Price, "Earning their Spurs," *Fort Worth Star-Telegram*, May 18, 2003.

8. Art Garcia, "Nash's world," *Fort Worth Star-Telegram*, August 27, 2003.

CHAPTER 8. SHARING HIS WEALTH

1. Art Garcia, "Nash's world," *Fort Worth Star-Telegram*, August 27, 2003.

2. Neil Davidson, "Nash is NBA's top athlete," *Montreal Gazette*, December 27, 2002.

3. Charles Foran, "The World According to Nash," *Toro Magazine*, November 2005.

4. James Deacon, "Maverick Nash," *Maclean's*, March 10, 2003.

5. Skip Bayless, "Nash unfit for court of public opinion," *San Jose Mercury News*, March 24, 2003.

6. *Seattle Times* news services, "Mavericks' players anti-war talk irks Spurs' Robinson," March 22, 2003.

7. Gwen Knapp, "Mavs' Nash throws caution to wind on impending war," *San Francisco Chronicle*, March 16, 2003.

8. Michael Farber, "My Sportsman Choice: Steve Nash," *Sports Illustrated*, November 2, 2005.

9. Steve Buffery, "MVP," *Toronto Sun*, January 30, 2005.

10. Richard Hoffer, "The Tao of Steve," *Sports Illustrated*, December 17, 2001.

11. Charles Foran, "The World According to Nash," *Toro Magazine*, November 2005.

12. Charles Barkley, "Steve Nash," *Time*, April 30, 2006.

13. Ibid.

CHAPTER 9. BACK WITH THE SUNS

1. Richie Whitt, "Despite the Mavs' demise, don't look for many changes," *Fort Worth Star-Telegram*, May 1, 2004.

2. Sean Deveney, "The Suns rise on Steve Nash," *The Sporting News*, December 6, 2004.

3. Dwain Price, "Return will likely be a point well taken," *Fort Worth Star-Telegram*, November 16, 2004.

4. Ibid.

5. Dwain Price, "END OF AN ERA," *Fort Worth Star-Telegram*, July 4, 2004.

6. Ibid.

7. Art Garcia, "Former Mav has new life in Phoenix," *Fort Worth Star-Telegram*, February 17, 2005.

8. Steve Buffery, "MVP," *Toronto Sun*, January 30, 2005.

9. Frank Isola, "Nash Bridges," *New York Daily News*, May 22, 2005.

9. Randy Galloway, "Former Mav a money player on and off court," *Fort Worth Star-Telegram*, May 21, 2005.

10. Frank Isola, "Nash Bridges," *New York Daily News*, May 22, 2005.

11. Art Garcia, "Monster Nash," *Fort Worth Star-Telegram*, May 21 2005.

12. Eddie Sefko, "Nash edges out O'Neal for MVP," *Dallas Morning News*, May 9, 2005.

CHAPTER 10. STILL COMPETING FOR AN NBA TITLE

1. Dan Bickley, "Suns laugh last," *Arizona Republic*, May 7, 2006.

2. NBA.com. "Post-Game Quotes," Western Conference Semifinals, Game 7: Suns 127, Clippers 107 <http://www.nba.com/suns/playoffs/quotes_060522.html> November 2, 2006..

3. Paola Boivin, "Camaraderie is Suns' biggest success," *Arizona Republic*, June 4, 2006.

4. Mike Tulumello, "Fatigue catches up to Nash, Suns," *East Valley Tribune*, June 4, 2006.

5. Dan Bickley, "Suns' magic run is over," *Arizona Republic*, June 4, 2006.

GLOSSARY

assist—A pass that leads to a basket.

charity—An organization that gives to the needy.

contract—A written agreement between a player and a team stating how much the player will be paid and for how long he will play for the team.

draft—An ordered selection process for pro sports teams to pick players from college, high school, and foreign pro leagues.

field goal—A made basket other than a free throw.

free throw—A shot awarded to a player who is fouled. Also called a foul shot.

Olympics—A competition involving countries from all over the world in different sports. The Olympics are held every four years for both summer and winter sports.

playoffs—A series of games between teams that had the best records in the NBA during the regular season. The NBA seeds eight teams into the playoffs in each of its two conferences, in order of their records. There are four rounds of the NBA Playoffs.

point guard—The position on a basketball team of the player responsible for running the offense, usually passing to teammates and shooting when necessary.

rebound—The act of gaining possession of a missed field goal or free-throw attempt.

scholarship—An agreement between a college and a student allowing that student to play a sport at the college and attend the college for free.

FOR MORE INFORMATION

FURTHER READING

Aron, Jaime. *Tales from the Dallas Mavericks*. Champaign, Ill.: Sports Publishing, 2003.

Rud, Jeff. *Long Shot: Steve Nash's Journey to the NBA*. Vancouver, B.C.: Polestar Books, 1996.

ON DVD

Steve Nash MVP Basketball: Fundamentals of Basketball. Varsity Films, 2005.

Steve Nash's 20 Minute Real Time Basketball Workout. Varsity Films, 2005.

WEB LINKS

Steve Nash's profile on NBA.com:
http://www.nba.com/playerfile/steve_nash/

Phoenix Suns' team page on NBA.com:
http://www.nba.com/suns

Steve Nash's profile on Basketball-Reference.com:
http://basketball-reference.com/players/n/nashst01.html

Steve Nash's home page:
http://www.stevenashmvp.com/stevenash/

The Steve Nash Foundation:
http://www.stevenash.org/html/main.html

INDEX

J

Jackson, Bobby, 70

Jamison, Antawn, 42, 87, 88, 98

Johnson, Avery, 88, 98, 110

Johnson, Kevin, 31, 33, 34–35, 36, 37

K

Katz, Mike, 26

Kerr, Steve, 74

Kidd, Jason, 27, 33, 34–35, 36, 37, 38

Kimble, Bo, 17, 19

Knapp, Gwen, 83–84

L

LaFrentz, Raef, 28, 42, 88

Los Angeles Clippers, 5, 6, 8, 42, 63, 105, 107–108

Los Angeles Lakers, 6, 8, 31, 36, 60, 72, 105, 106–107

M

MacCulloch, Todd, 51, 52

Malone, Karl, 18, 56

Manning, Danny, 36

Marbury, Stephon, 30, 31

Marion, Shawn, 9, 39, 95, 103, 105

McCain, John, 86

Memphis Grizzlies, 78, 98

Mills, Chris, 22

Minnesota Timberwolves, 31, 54, 64, 88

T

Terry, Jason, 98

Thomas, Kurt, 103, 104

Thomas, Tim, 103, 104, 107

Tottenham Hotspur, 12, 13

Traylor, Robert, 42

Triano, Jay, 52, 53

U

Utah Jazz, 18, 54, 56–60, 62

V

Van Exel, Nick, 63–64, 74, 83, 87, 88, 98

Van Horn, Keith, 98

Vaught, Loy, 10

W

Walker, Antoine, 87, 88, 98

Wallace, Rasheed, 68

Webber, Chris, 65, 70

West Coast Conference, 17–19, 21, 22, 24, 25, 26, 27

Y

YMCA, 80